George Forbes

The transit of Venus

George Forbes

The transit of Venus

ISBN/EAN: 9783743330474

Manufactured in Europe, USA, Canada, Australia, Japa

Cover: Foto ©ninafisch / pixelio.de

George Forbes

The transit of Venus

THE TRANSIT OF VENUS.

BY

GEORGE FORBES, B.A.,

WITH NUMEROUS ILLUSTRATIONS.

London and New York:
MACMILLAN AND CO.
1874

[*The Right of Translation and Reproduction is reserved.*]

PREFACE.

The following pages, revised from a series of articles published in NATURE, are based upon a paper originally read before the Philosophical Society of Glasgow, in 1873. I believe that I have performed the duty of the historian with impartiality. I have done my best to make the technicalities comprehensible. The account of the preparations of different nations is as complete as it was in my power to make it.

My best thanks are due to Mr. W. H. M. Christie, of the Royal Observatory, Greenwich, for having kindly undertaken to revise the proofs during my absence from England.

GEORGE FORBES.

S.S. "Illimani."
June 3, 1874.

	PAGE
CHAPTER I.	1
CHAPTER II.	15
CHAPTER III.	29
CHAPTER IV.	46
CHAPTER V.	60
CHAPTER VI.	75
CHAPTER VII.	89

LIST OF ILLUSTRATIONS.

FIG.	PAGE
1	2
2	4
3	6
4	7
5	7
6	11
7	13
8	16
9	18
10	25
11	30
12	36
13	38
14	39
15	49
16	51
17.—Lord Lindsay's Photographic arrangements as set up at Dun Echt	57
18.—The transit-instrument of the British Expedition	69
19.—Portable Altazimuth Instrument	71
20.—Equatorial of the British Expedition	81
21.—Photo-heliograph of the British Expeditions	97

THE
TRANSIT OF VENUS.

CHAPTER I.

IN days of old it was supposed that the earth held the central position of the solar system, and that moon, sun, and planets moved round it, each in its own orbit. The moon was supposed to be nearest to us, then came Venus, then Mercury, after that the sun, then Mars, Jupiter, and Saturn. We now know that of all these the moon is the only one which revolves round the earth, and that all the planets travel round the sun in paths at different distances from it in the following order, the first being that nearest the sun :— Mercury, Venus, the Earth, Mars, Jupiter, Saturn. These are all the planets which were known to the ancients. Since Mercury and Venus were formerly supposed to be lower than the sun, and all the others higher, the name of *inferior planets* was given to the former, and *superior planets* to the others. These terms are still retained by astronomers, though the ideas that gave rise to these terms are long since exploded. Fig. 1 shows the appearances presented by

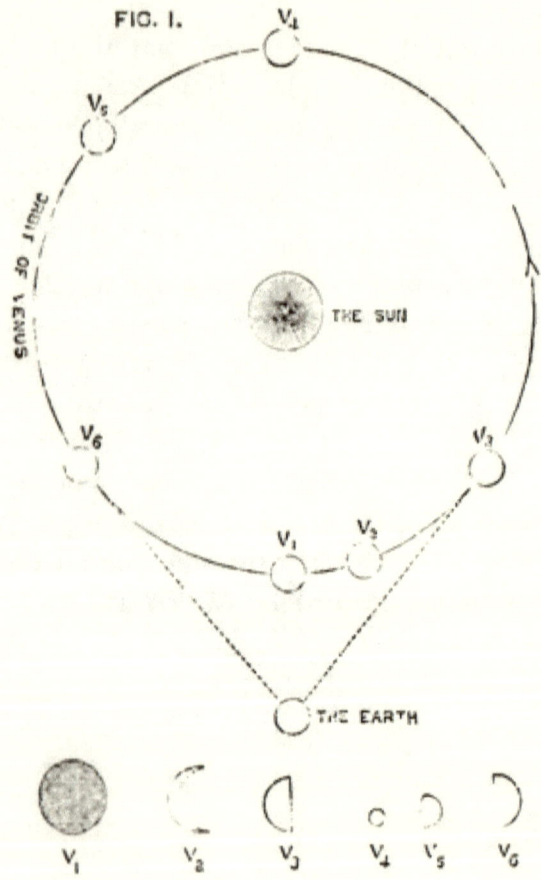

Venus, one of the inferior planets, in the course of its journey round the sun. V is the planet. E is the earth, which is shown in the figure always in one position, although of course it also describes an orbit

round the sun. We are naturally led by a study of the diagram to three points of interest concerning the motions of an inferior planet.

The first is that the planet can never seem to be far distant from the sun. Venus moves round the sun in the direction shown by the arrow. The earth rotates in the same direction. We are supposed to be looking down upon the solar system from some point in the northern heavens. It will be noticed that when the planet leaves the point V_1, she will seem to recede from the sun more and more, until she reaches the position V_3. She can never appear further from the sun than this, and is then said to be at her greatest eastern elongation. She then approaches the direction in which the sun is seen, until she is lost in the brightness of his rays. During all the time she is seen best in the early morning before sunrise, setting before the sun. When Venus has passed this position her distance from the sun appears to an observer upon the earth to increase until she reaches V_6, her greatest western elongation, when she again begins to approach the sun.

The next point to be noticed is that she is sometimes a great deal closer to the earth than at others; and when she is nearest to the earth she appears to be largest. At her closest approach to the earth she is only about 26,000,000 miles away; but when farthest off her distance is 158,000,000 miles. Her apparent size is therefore much greater in the first case than in the second. These differences are shown at the lower part of Fig. 1.

The third point to be mentioned is that she exhibits phases just as the moon does. In any position that hemisphere alone is illuminated which is directed to the sun; so that in the position V_3, when we can only see one-half of that hemisphere, she will have the appearance of a half-moon. So in the position V_2 she has a crescent form, and at V_5 a gibbous one. The apparent size and shape of the planet in its different positions are shown in the lower part of Fig. 1.

The question now arises, what will happen when Venus is between us and the sun? In the first place, since her illuminated hemisphere is turned away from us, she will be invisible indeed; we shall have no chance of seeing her, unless she be seen as a black spot upon the bright surface of the sun. We should naturally expect that this would happen every time that the planet is at its least distance from us. A simple consideration shows that this need not be the case. The orbits of Venus and the earth do not lie in the same plane. In other words, we cannot represent accurately the paths of Venus and the earth by a drawing upon a sheet of paper. The orbit of Venus would have to be tilted up above the plane of

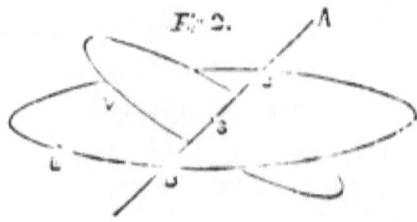

Fig. 2.

the earth's orbit. Both of these planes pass through the sun, but they are inclined to each other at a certain small angle. This will be seen by a glance at Fig. 2, where V represents the orbit of Venus, E that of the earth. The line A B, which passes through the sun is called the line of nodes; and it is quite clear that in order to see Venus as a black spot upon the sun, both the Earth and Venus must lie approximately on this line of nodes. Now it generally happens that when Venus is at her least distance from the Earth, these two planets occupy some such places as V and E, so that she seems to be above the sun; and, as the illuminated side is turned away from us, she is invisible. Only twice in a century does she reach the node, so nearly at the same time as the earth, as to be seen as a black spot upon the sun. Such a phenomenon is called a Transit of Venus. If it happen that Venus seems to pass across the centre of the sun she takes about eight hours to complete the passage. The earth occupies the position A always in June, and the position B in December. If there be a transit of Venus when the earth is at B, Venus is said to be at the *descending* node, because then she is descending from the northern portion of her orbit to the southern. When Venus is at C she is at her *ascending* node.

It has been said that there are, roughly speaking, two transits of Venus in a century. The following table shows all the transits of which we know anything:—

    1631. Predicted by Kepler, but not observed.
    1639. Predicted and observed by Horrox.
    1761. Predicted by Halley; observed by many
    1769. Observed generally.
    1874.
    1882.

It will be noticed that the transits occur in pairs

eight years apart; the reason of this can easily be rendered clear. The earth takes 365·256 days to go round the sun; Venus takes only 224·7 days. Suppose then that at any particular date Venus and the earth are at the node simultaneously, viz. at V and E, Fig. 3; a transit of Venus over the sun's disc

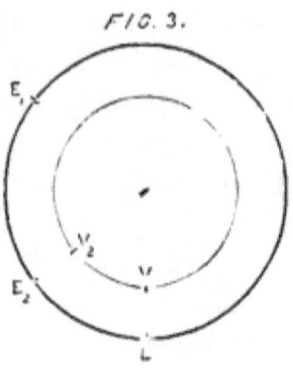

FIG. 3.

will be seen. When Venus has completed a revolution the earth will have moved away to E_1, and Venus will not overtake the earth until they reach the positions V_2 and E_2. This is 583·920 days from the time when they were at V and E; but V_2 and E_2 do not lie upon the line of nodes; hence there can be no transit. After another 584 days Venus will again be in conjunction with the sun, but still not on the line of nodes. But the fifth conjunction occurs after 2919·6 days (5×583·920); and the earth completes eight revolutions in 2922·05 days. Thus it appears that, at this conjunction of Venus with the sun, the earth and Venus are very near to their old positions V and E. Hence they are almost on the line of nodes. In this case we can without difficulty examine the possibility of a transit. If we suppose the motion of the earth to be stopped, the apparent motions of the sun and Venus may be represented as in Fig 4, where a portion of the orbit of Venus where it cuts the ecliptic near the

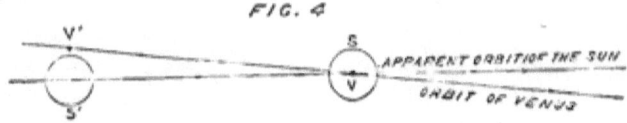

FIG. 4

nodes is shown. When the sun and Venus are on the line of nodes simultaneously s represents the sun and v Venus. At the fifth conjunction the sun will not quite have reached s, but will be $2\frac{1}{2}$ days behind at s'; Venus will then be at v'. Now in this case there can be no transit visible, for here Venus is quite out of range of the sun. But if in the original transit the sun was a little past the node as at s (Fig. 5), then eight years after he will be at s', and there will be another

FIG. 5

transit. It follows from this that there will be a pair of transits eight years apart, only when in the first one Venus does not pass close to the sun's centre. This equality of eight revolutions of the earth, with thirteen of Venus, is very interesting, because this fact was shown by the present Astronomer Royal to account for an inequality in the earth's motion due to the attracting influence of Venus. The result of a short calculation informs us that for positions of Venus and the earth near the line of nodes, Venus is at one conjunction 22' 16" distant from her position at the conjunction which occurred eight years previously,[1] this distance being measured at right angles to the ecliptic. Now the sun's diameter is 32'. This shows why, generally, there are two transits eight years apart.

The first prediction of a transit of Venus was made by Kepler,[2] and was calculated from his Rudolphine tables. In 1631, the year predicted, astronomers of Europe were eagerly on the watch for so rare a spectacle. But the calculation was in error, so that it took place when the sun was below the horizon in Europe, and was consequently invisible.

After this no astronomers seem to have interested themselves about the possibility of such an occurrence, with one exception—Jeremiah Horrox, a curate of the village of Hoole, near Liverpool, who was much devoted to astronomical pursuits.[3] He possessed some tables for calculating the places of the planets; but his observations did not agree at all with them. He had, however, before discovering the faults of

[1] For at the fifth conjunction the earth is 2·45 days distant from her place at the original conjunction. This is equivalent to 2° 24' 59", when viewed from the sun, from which subtract 2' 44" (= the retrogression of the node of Venus in eight years), and we have 2° 22' 15" = the angular distance of the earth from its corrected original position, as seen from the sun. The ratio of this to the angular distance of Venus from her original position as seen from the earth = $\frac{\text{dist. of Venus from earth}}{\text{dist. of Venus from sun}} = \frac{277}{723}$. Multiplying 2° 22' 15" by 723, and dividing by 277, we have 6° 11' 17". Multiplying this by ·06 = tan 3° 23' 3.", which is the inclination of the orbit of Venus, we have 22' 16" = the latitude of Venus at the fifth conjunction.

[2] "Admonitiuncula ad Curiosos Rerum Cœlestium," Leipsic, 1626.

[3] See *Nature*, vol. viii. p. 113.

Lansberg's tables, calculated from them the future positions of the planets. This work, with corrections deduced from his own observations, led him to predict a transit of Venus, visible in England, for the year 1639. He acquainted his friend Crabtree, of Manchester, with the results of his calculation, and then prepared himself for the observation. He considered the best method to be the employment of a telescope to throw an image of the sun on a white sheet of paper in a darkened room. A circle was drawn, of about 6 inches diameter, upon the paper, to make the sun's image exactly fill the circle. A plumb-line would give him the direction of the vertical, and by marking successive positions of the planet on the sun's disc, he would be able to calculate many of the elements of Venus. Such an observation is of course peculiarly well suited for determining the diameter of the planet, the inclination of its orbit, the position of the node, and the true time of passing this node. His calculation showed that the transit ought to commence on the afternoon of November 24 (old style); but to guard against disappointment, and because of discrepancies in various tables, he kept a watch from the 23rd. On returning from some clerical duties on the 24th (Sunday) he was gratified by beholding a black spot on the sheet of paper, which indicated the presence of Venus on the sun's disc. He made three observations before sunset and has left us a drawing to illustrate the observations.[1]

It is curious to find an astronomer supporting the opinions of the astrologers; but in his treatise we

---
[1] Venus in Sole Visa.

find that the chance of a clouded atmosphere caused him much anxiety, for Jupiter and Mercury were in conjunction with the sun almost at the same time as Venus. This seemed to him to forebode great severity of weather. He adds, "Mercury, whose conjunction with the sun is invariably attended with storm and tempest, was especially to be feared. In this apprehension I coincide with the opinion of the astrologers, because it is confirmed by experience; but in other respects I cannot help despising their more than puerile vanities." But we must not laugh at Horrox for his opinion. In our own day there is a considerable number of diligent astronomers who believe that the cyclones in the Indian Ocean, certain other winds, the growth of vines, and various other phenomena, are in part regulated by the positions of Venus and Jupiter with respect to the sun.[1]

Horrox's observations have been of great value in perfecting the tables of Venus. He was further led by a kind of analogy, much in vogue at the time, to deduce from his observations a value of the sun's distance from the earth. It will readily be understood that if we could find out what size, in angular measure the earth would seem to have if viewed from the sun, we should have a means of determining how much greater the distance from the earth to the sun is than the diameter of the earth. For, suppose s (Fig. 6) to be the position of an observer placed upon the sun,

---

[1] See the researches of Messrs. De la Rue, Stewart, and Loewy on the connection of sun-spot frequency with planetary positions. "Phil. Trans."; also the writings of Mr. Meldrum, Mr. E. J. Stone, Prof. Balfour Stewart, M. Poey, and others, on the connection between terrestrial phenomena and sun-spot frequency.

S L, S M the directions in which he must look to see the opposite sides of the earth, so that the inclination of these lines is known. All we have to do now is to draw a circle of any size and move it about between

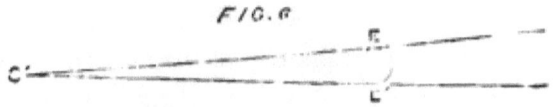

FIG. 6

the lines S L, S M, until it just fills the interval, as at E E'. If now we measure with a ruler how much greater S E is than E E' we shall know the distance from the earth to the sun, the earth's diameter being taken as the unit of measurement; and if we multiply this by the diameter of the earth measured in miles we shall know the distance from the earth to the sun, in miles. All that we require to know is the size of the angle E S E'. Horrox estimated the probable value of this angle in the following manner. From the observations of Tycho Brahé it appeared that during the transit of Venus the apparent diameter of the planet would be 12′ 18″; while Lansberg found 12′ 21″; and Kepler 6′ 51″. Horrox found from his measurements that it was only 1′ 16″. The error of ordinary observations arises from the apparent enlargement of the planet's disc through irradiation. Gassendi had in the same manner, during the transit of Mercury in 1631, reduced the apparent diameter of Mercury to scarcely 20″. From these data it can be found that the apparent diameters of Venus and Mercury as seen from the sun would be 21″ and 34″ respectively. Proceeding to the other planets he arrived at the general conclusion that each of them would, if viewed from the sun, have an apparent diameter of about 28". Applying this to the case of the earth, he showed that the distance of the earth from the sun must be 7,500 diameters of the earth (it may be well here to state that the latest measurements show the apparent diameter of the earth as viewed from the sun to be about 18", and the distance=11,400 diameters). This analogy by Horrox gave a much closer approach to the truth than previous conjectures.

Before taking leave of Horrox, we must say a few words on his work. Although he died at the early age of 23, during his career he showed a remarkable aptitude for the acquisition of knowledge, and for the striking out of new ideas. He lived at a time when the scientific spirit of the age was leading up to the theory of gravitation, and many passages in his writings show that he had even then grasped the grand idea of the theory, and that he was well fitted to become its constructor and its expounder. His researches on the lunar and planetary theories also indicate his great genius.

We have already mentioned some of the uses to which careful observations of a transit of Venus may be applied ; viz. the correction of the elements of the planet's orbit. But the observation also leads us to a knowledge of the distance of the sun from the earth, and in a manner much more direct and logical than that employed by Horrox. There is an opinion very prevalent that a transit of Venus affords the best means of determining this distance. So far as our present knowledge goes we are hardly justified in such a statement until after the observations that shall be made in the present year.

Before entering upon the method by which we measure the sun's distance, let us devote a few lines to explaining what is meant by the word *parallax*, which is continually employed in such discussions. Let a man stand in a street exactly north of a lamp-post. The lamp-post will seem to be south of him. Now let him cross over to the other side of the street. The lamp-post will now be in some other direction, such as south-west. This movement of the direction of the lamp-post is the effect of parallax. Now let us suppose, by a stretch of imagination, that a man observes the moon from the centre of the earth. He will see it in the direction C M (Fig. 7). If now he goes to A he will see it in the direction A M. The

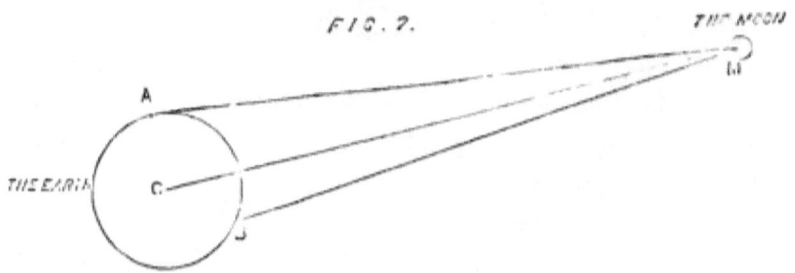

FIG. 7.

angle A M C through which the moon appears to have been moved is the parallax of the moon as observed from A. It will be noticed that the parallax is an error introduced into the observed position of the moon, and which must be allowed for if we wish to get the position as seen from C. Moreover, the parallax at B is different from what it is at A. But at no point on the surface of the earth can the parallax be greater than at A. And if we know the parallax of the moon at A, we can deduce that at B from a knowledge of the relative positions of A, B, and C. Hence it is useful to have a distinct name for the parallax at A. Now it will be noticed that a line drawn from C to A is the vertical line at A; hence the moon M will appear to be on the horizon to an observer at A; and hence the moon has its greatest parallax when on the horizon. For this reason the parallax at A is called the moon's *horizontal parallax*. Further, since the equatorial diameter of the earth is greater than the polar, the parallax will be greater, when the moon is on the horizon, to an observer at the equator than to an observer at one of the poles. Hence the greatest parallax we can have occurs when the moon is on the horizon and the observer is at the equator; this value of the parallax is the *equatorial horizontal parallax*. In the same way the sun has an equatorial horizontal parallax, and if we knew its value we could find out the sun's distance from the earth as explained above (Fig. 6).

CHAPTER II.

There is perhaps no problem which has been so constant a source of interest to the learned in all ages as the solving of the mystery of the solar system. The labours of Copernicus, Tycho Brahé, Kepler, and Newton have given us a general knowledge of the nature of the planetary motions; and the investigations of later mathematicians have enabled us to predict, with wonderful accuracy, the future positions of the planets. But the dimensions of the solar system are not known with the same precision.

It is true that we know the *relative* distances of all the planets from the sun with tolerable exactness. This problem has been attacked by two totally different methods. The first consists in measuring directly the changes that are produced in the motions of the planets when the earth has moved through a certain portion of its orbit. In the case of the planets Mercury and Venus, which move in smaller orbits than that of the earth, the direct observation can easily be made. For let us suppose VV' and EE

(Fig. 8) to be the orbits of Venus and the Earth, and s to be the sun. Let us watch the position of Venus night after night until she is as far away from the sun as possible. If we measure her apparent distance from the sun by astronomical means, we shall

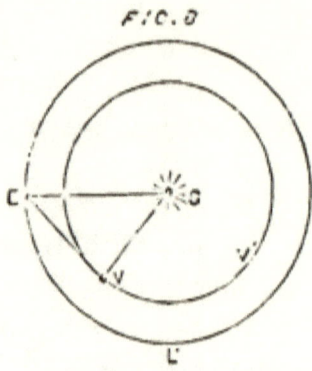

FIG. 8

know that the Sun, Venus, and the Earth occupy positions such as S, V, and E; the directions E S and E V being known from our observations. By measuring off the distances S V and S E on the diagram, we actually find the relation between the earth's distance from the sun and that of Venus. The same can be done with Mercury; but for the superior planets the direct mode of observation is more difficult.

But there is an indirect method which is much more easy to apply. Kepler's three laws have been shown to be necessary consequences of Newton's theory of gravitation. Now Kepler's third law tells us how to find the relative distances of two planets from the sun when we know the relation between their periods of revolution. The exact law is this: — Multiply the number of years taken by a planet to go round the sun, by the same number. This gives us a first number. Then find a second number which, multiplied by itself twice, gives us the first number; this second number is the distance of the planet from the sun (the earth's distance being called 1). To take an example: Jupiter takes about 11 years to go round the sun; 11 multiplied by 11 gives us a first number, 121. Now if 5 be multiplied by 5 we get 25, and if this be again multiplied by 5 we get 125, which is almost the same as the first number, 121. Hence we are right in saying that Jupiter is about five times as far from the sun as the earth is. If we had used the exact number of years we should have got the exact distance. Now it is very easy to find the period of revolution of a planet. For we can easily measure the interval between two dates when Jupiter and the Earth, for example, are in the same line with the sun; in other words, we can measure the "synodical revolution" of Jupiter; and from this it is easy to calculate the time of Jupiter's revolution round the sun.

By applying these methods to all the planets we can lay down their orbits upon a plan; *all we wish now is to find the scale upon which our plan is drawn.* If we knew the distance of the earth from the sun, or if we knew the distance between any two of the planetary orbits, we should know the scale upon which our plan is laid down. Various methods have been adopted for this, but the one which makes use of a transit of Venus has generally been considered to be the most accurate.

One method which has successfully been applied to

measuring the moon's distance is that used by surveyors. The surveyor chooses two spots, B, C, whose distance he measures. Suppose it to be one mile. He represents this distance, say, by a line one inch long on a sheet of paper. He then takes a telescope, mounted so as to enable him to measure any angle through which it is turned. He places the telescope at B, pointing towards C. He then turns it till it points at the distant object, and finds what the angle of B is. He then draws the line B A upon the paper, and he knows that the distant object lies somewhere on the line B A. He then does the same with C, and thus he knows that the remote object lies on C A. But A is the only point lying both on B A and C A; hence C corresponds to the distant object. If on measuring C A he finds it to be 30 inches, then since C B, which is 1 inch, means 1 mile; C A, which is 30 inches, means 30 miles, and this is what he wanted to find out.

If, instead of taking a base-line (as it is called) of one mile, the diameter of the earth, or 8,000 miles,

FIG. 9.

be taken; then, if the moon be the distant object, we can determine its distance in almost the same way. It is in this manner that the moon's distance has been measured. It is easy to see that if the angle at A (Fig. 9) were very small, a slight error in measuring either of the angles B or C would make a great difference in the distance deduced for the remote object. Hence, if the moon's parallax were not large, this method would be unsuitable. The parallax of the sun is very small, and hence we cannot find the sun's distance with any exactness by this method.

But if any one of the planets ever came so close to the earth as to make its parallax tolerably large, then we could determine the scale upon which the solar system is built up. Now Venus and Mars are two planets which at certain times come closer to the Earth than any other planet does. But, unfortunately, when Venus is nearest the earth she is generally invisible, because the whole of her illuminated side is turned away from us. Mars, however, is a planet that gives us a very favourable opportunity for determining its distance. The advantage is increased by this peculiarity, that every fifteen years Mars is at its shortest distance from the sun, at the same time that the earth is at its greatest distance, the two planets being also in the same line with the sun, so that they are closer than we might have thought possible. In fact, on these occasions Mars is nearer to the earth by $\frac{1}{5}$th part than she is if the conjunction take place when both the earth and Mars are at about their mean distances from the sun. Suppose then that under such circumstances two observers, one at Greenwich and the other at the Cape of Good Hope (where there is a fine observatory), observe the position of Mars as compared with that of a star at the same time. The position of Mars will be displaced by parallax; and by comparing the apparent angular distance of the planet from the fixed star at these two places we can find the sum of the parallaxes in these cases. Hence we can find the distance of Mars, as already explained.

This was the method which first gave a value of the solar parallax with anything like accuracy. At the suggestion of Cassini, the French sent out an expedition to the Cape, under the astronomer Picard. The value obtained for the sun's parallax was 9″5. Prof. Henderson in 1836, and Mr. Stone in 1862, utilised this method. Another opportunity will occur in 1877.

Before proceeding to the method of the Transits of Venus, it will be well briefly to allude to some other methods by means of which the solar parallax, or the sun's distance, has been estimated.

It has been found that light takes a sensible time to propagate itself through space. Hence, when one of Jupiter's satellites passes into the shadow of the planet, this fact is not communicated to our vision for something like 38 minutes, the time taken by light to pass from Jupiter to the Earth. Now, when we are on the same side of the sun as Jupiter, this distance is shorter by the whole diameter of the earth's orbit than when we are at the opposite side of the sun. Hence, in the former case, the eclipses will seem to take place sooner than the predicted time, and in the latter case later. The difference in either case is about 8 minutes, and as we know that light travels over 298,500 kilometres per second,[1] this tells us

[1] As determined by Foucault, *Comptes Rendus de l'Acad. des Sciences*, vol. lv. p. 502; also by Cornu, *Comptes Rendus*, Feb. 10, 1873.

that our distance from the sun is about 91,000,000 miles.

But our knowledge of the velocity of light has been utilised in another manner to solve the same problem. You see that if we know the earth's velocity in miles, we can find its distance from the sun. For if it goes 1½ million miles in one day, it must go over 365 times that in a year, and *that measures in miles the circumference of our earth's orbit*, and hence we can get our distance from the sun. How then are we to find the velocity of the earth in miles? This depends on a curious property of light. In a steady down-pour of rain you hold your umbrella upright if you are standing still, but incline it forward if you are walking fast. This is to make the umbrella catch the rain-drops. The amount of inclination you give it depends upon the rate at which you are walking compared with the velocity with which the drops fall. The same thing happens with light. We have to incline our telescopes forward a little in the direction in which the earth is moving to catch the rays of light; and at opposite seasons of the year the earth is moving in contrary directions, and the telescope has to be pointed in sensibly different directions. The inclination that a telescope receives is known, and the velocity of light being known, we can find the velocity of the earth, and hence, as I have shown, the distance of the earth from the sun.

There is another method of peculiar interest depending upon the motions of the moon. The law of gravitation says that the attraction of any body for any other one depends upon the distance between them.

The moon is attracted to the earth by a force, depending upon the distance of the moon, which is known in miles. But the moon is caused to deviate from its natural course on account of the sun's attraction. This depends upon the distance of the sun from the earth, and if this be not known exactly in miles we shall see that it is impossible to apply calculation to foretell the motions of the moon; for, if upon any scale we attempt to lay down upon paper the relative positions of the sun, earth, and moon, we shall place the moon at its proper distance, and the sun, though in its proper direction, will not be placed at the proper distance, and we shall not know the direction in which it attracts the moon, nor the magnitude of this attraction, and we shall make our calculation wrongly, and the moon's observed place will differ considerably from its calculated place.

Such a difference was actually detected by the illustrious Hansen, whose tables of the moon are the best we possess. Hansen saw that this must be due to a wrong assumption as to the distance of the sun, and communicated his doubts to the Astronomer Royal[1] in the year 1854. This led to a re-discussion of our knowledge of the subject which has confirmed Hansen's views, and which leads us to see the importance of knowing accurately the sun's distance, if we wish ever to have our tables of the moon so accurate that we may determine the longitude by their aid. This method for investigating the solar parallax was first used by Laplace.[2]

[1] *Month'y Notices, R. A. S.*, vol. xv., Nov. 1854.
[2] *Système du Monde*, t. ii. p. 91.

More recently, M. le Verrier has suggested a new method that promises in time to be the best.[1] In the lunar theory, an equation appears connecting the relative masses of the earth and sun with the solar parallax, so that if we know the one we can find the other; and from a peculiarity in the equations, a small error in determining the relative masses will affect only very slightly the deduced parallax. Le Verrier finds the ratio of the masses of the earth and sun by determining the effect of the earth's attraction upon Venus and Mars. This being applied to the lunar theory, a value of the solar parallax is obtained.

The method, however, which has found most favour up to the present time, is the employing of transits of Venus to measure the sun's distance. When a transit of Venus occurs, the first evidence of the phenomenon is given by a slight notch being made in the contour of the sun's edge at a certain spot. This notch increases until the full form of the planet is seen. The first appearance of a notch is called the time of first external contact. But when the planet appears to be wholly on the sun, her black figure is still connected with the sun's limb by a sort of black ligament, of which we shall say more hereafter. When the whole of the planet is just inside the sun's edge, the time of first internal contact has arrived. The breaking of the ligament is a very definite occurrence, and was, until lately, taken to indicate the true moment of internal contact. The second internal and external contacts take place as the planet leaves the sun.

[1] *Comptes Rendus*, July 22, 1872.

In 1663, the celebrated James Gregory, in his famous work the "Optica Promota," *prop.* 87, *Scholium*, alludes to the possibility of determining the sun's parallax by means of the transit of an inferior planet. He has been showing methods of finding the parallax of a planet by comparison of observations made at different parts of the earth upon the position of the planet compared with that of a star. He then takes, in place of a fixed star, another planet, the two being in one line, as seen from the earth. The application of this to the case of Mercury or Venus and the sun, was obvious.

But Halley was the first to see clearly what a powerful means of determining the sun's parallax an observation of contact really is. So far as I can discover, he first mentions the method in a letter to Sir Jonas Moore, written at St. Helena in 1677,[1] just after having seen a transit of Mercury. The exactness with which he believed the time of contact to be determinable, led him frequently afterwards to urge his countrymen to make every effort to utilise the method on the occasion of the transits of 1761 and 1769, when he should be dead.[2] And thus, in addition to his celebrated prediction of a comet, he left a second legacy to his successors, who, as Englishmen, might be entitled to be proud of his foresight though he could not live to reap the glory of it.

It is a matter of some difficulty to show, in an elementary manner, the way in which the value of the sun's parallax can be found from observation of

[1] Hooke's "Lectures and Collections," 1678.
[2] "Catalogus Stellarum Australium;" also "Phil. Trans." 1694 and 1715.

contact. We will try, however, to put it in a light which anyone, with a little attention, will understand.

1. It must be thoroughly understood, from what has already been said, that if we know the amount of the sun's parallax; in other words, if we know the angle subtended by any known distance on the earth's surface, at the sun, we know the sun's distance.

2. We know that the relative positions of the earth, Venus, and the sun, are given by supposing the earth

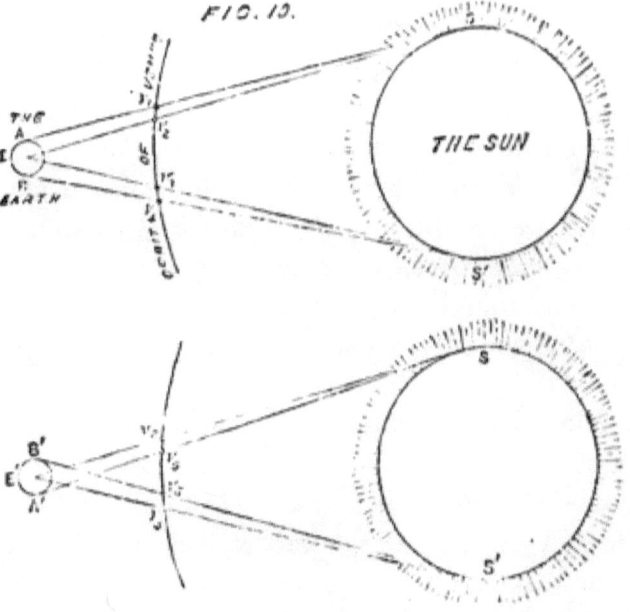

FIG. 13.

to go round the sun in 365 days, and Venus in 224 days. Or, if we please, we may take no account of the earth's revolution, but suppose it fixed, in which case the revolution of Venus *relatively* to the earth (*i.e.* the synodical revolution) is 584 days.

3. If, then, Venus moves round the sun through 360° relatively to the earth in 584 days, she moves through $\frac{1}{584}$ of that in one day, and through $\frac{360}{584 \times 24}$ of a degree in one hour; which is at the rate of about $1\frac{1}{3}$ second of arc in a minute of time.

Now we are ready to understand Halley's reasoning.

Let A (Fig. 10) be the position of an observer on the earth at the time of first internal contact. S is the sun, and V_1 is now the position of Venus. This observer sees the contact earlier than a hypothetical observer at the earth's centre would see it, by the time Venus takes to move over $V_1 V_2$. If we knew by calculation the instant when an observer at E would see it, and the observer at A saw it 8 minutes sooner, then, since Venus moves over $1\frac{1}{5}''$ in a minute, she has moved over $8 \times 1\frac{1}{5}$ or $9\frac{3}{5}''$ of arc in this time, and hence we learn that the angle A S E = $9\frac{3}{5}''$.

Suppose that by the time of the last contact the point A on the earth's surface has been carried by her rotation to B: the time of the last contact will now be too late by 8 minutes; since the whole duration of the transit as seen by this observer is 16 minutes too long, and the angle moved over by Venus in 16 min. is the sum of the sun's parallax as seen from A and from B.

But we cannot calculate with absolute accuracy the duration a transit would have when seen from E, because we should require to know more accurately than we do the values of Venus' and the sun's diameters.

Halley got rid of this by taking another station

which should be in the position A at the beginning of the transit. In the case we have been considering the time of the first contact would here be too late by 8 minutes; and if this place had reached B' by the end of the transit, the time of contact would be too soon by 8 minutes. Hence in this case the whole duration would be shortened by 16 minutes; but in the former case it was lengthened by 16 minutes. Hence 32 minutes is the time taken by Venus to pass over an angle equal to the sum of the parallaxes in the four cases considered. This difference of duration, whether it be 32 minutes or anything else, is a quantity which can be observed. Now Venus moves over about $1\tfrac{1}{5}''$ of arc in a minute, or $38\tfrac{2}{5}''$ in these 32 minutes. Hence one-fourth of $38\tfrac{2}{5}''$ or $9\tfrac{3}{5}''$ would appear, from the above hypothetical observation, to be the value of Venus's parallax.

It must be noticed that we have here supposed that the transit takes exactly 12 hours, whereas the longest transit cannot exceed 8 hours. We have also supposed that two stations had been selected which were exactly situated so as to bring out the full effect of parallax at the time of each observation. These suppositions have been introduced only to simplify the explanation of the method. Anyone who has followed the above explanation will see how the method may be applied to actual cases that may occur.

Halley saw (what many people fail to see even now) that the great accuracy of the method consists in this, that in one second of time Venus moves over about $0''.02$; and if we can determine the time of ontact, with an error of no more than a second, we are measuring the sun's parallax with an error of no more than ·02 of a second of arc.

Halley even pointed out the best stations for observation. We may consider the earth to be at rest if we suppose Venus to move with the velocity she has relative to the earth. He supposed that the planet would cross near the sun's centre, and that the transit would occupy about eight hours. An observer in India would see the commencement of the transit four hours before mid-day, and the end of the transit four hours after mid-day. But, in the meantime, the part of the earth where he is has been moving from west to east, and Venus has moved from east to west, hence the duration of transit will have been shortened. But at Hudson's Bay the transit begins just before sunset and ends just after sunrise, that part of the earth having moved in mean time from east to west so as to lengthen the transit; and thus at one place the duration of transit is lengthened, and at the other shortened, and the difference of time depends upon the parallaxes of Venus and the sun[1] at the two stations, and after finding these parallaxes we can calculate the equatorial horizontal parallax.

[1] This lengthening and shortening of the time of transit will be rendered more evident by an analogy. A person standing still sees a carriage pass between him and a distant house. The carriage will take a certain time to pass the house. But if he also be moving, and in the same direction with the carriage, the transit of the carriage will take longer; but if he move in the opposite direction to the carriage, the transit will take a shorter time. If, then, two persons be seated at opposite sides of a merry-go-round, so that at the time the carriage seems to be passing the distant house, one observer is moving with the carriage and the other in the opposite direction; then one observer will see the time lengthened, and the other shortened. Now, the world is such a merry-go-round, and the positions of these two people correspond to the positions of India and Hudson's Bay, as pointed out by Halley.

CHAPTER III.

In the previous chapters various methods have been indicated by means of which we may discover the scale upon which the plan of the solar system is drawn. The last one concluded by illustrating the nature of the methods of employing a transit of Venus, as proposed by Halley. It will be noticed that this method can be utilised in the way there indicated only when Venus passes nearly along a diameter of the sun. Halley, in fact, founding his calculations upon erroneous data, was led to conclude that this would be the case in 1761. In this he erred, and another slight but important mistake having been made in his calculations, it followed that at Hudson's Bay, his northern station, the transit was invisible.

The present chapter will be devoted to a description of the methods to be employed in the coming transit for determining the solar parallax. In subsequent chapters the preparations which have actually been made for observing the transit of 1874 will be described; and the difficulties encountered in this kind of observation enumerated.

Let the reader now examine Fig. 11 and pay particular attention to the description of it, and he will thus be enabled to better understand what follows. The Earth, Venus, and the Sun are here represented in their relative positions; and lines are drawn to show the directions in which two observers at opposite sides of the earth will see Venus upon the solar disc. It follows from this that an observer on the southern

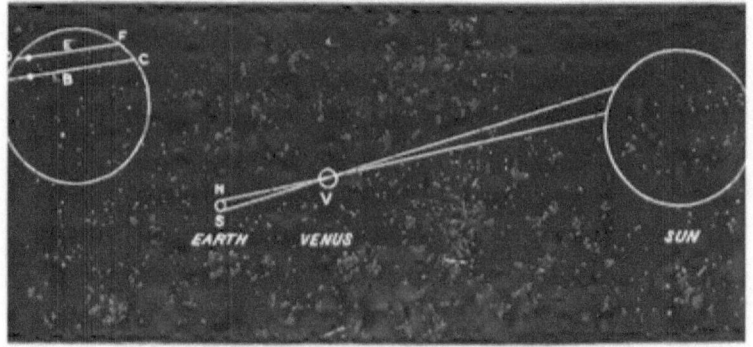

Fig. 11.

portion of the earth will see Venus trace a path D E F upon the sun's disc further north than the path A B C which a northern observer on the earth sees it trace. Now Venus will be three times as far from the sun as from the earth on that date. From this it follows that the distance between the two lines A B C and D E F will be three times as great as the distance N S. But the distance N S upon the earth can be easily found out. Suppose it to be 6,000 miles. In that case the distance between A B C and D E F is known to be 18,000 miles. But it needs no demonstration to convince us that if we have a distance of 18,000 miles measured out for us upon the sun's surface we can determine the distance of the sun from the earth.

Now the apparent distance between the two lines ABC and DEF is the least observed distances between Venus' centre and the sun's during the transit. *If, then, we can measure accurately the least distance between the centres of Venus and the sun, at two stations suitably chosen, we can determine the sun's distance.*

There are three methods by means of which this may be effected; the photographic method, the heliometric method, and the method of durations. We shall consider these in order.

I. *The Photographic Method.*—It is easy to see that by continuing during the transit, at each station, to take photographs of the sun, in which Venus will be represented as a black spot, these photographs may be so combined as to indicate definitely the apparent path of Venus as seen at each of these two stations. This method is looked forward to with much interest, because it is the first time that photography has been extensively employed in delicate astronomical measurements. It is not generally known how extremely accurate a means of observation photography is. We owe much to Mr. De la Rue, whose success in the application of photography to astronomy has been unequalled, for having given us a most clear account of what has been done in this way.[1] The method has been employed in America to measure the distances between double stars. The double star is photographed

---

[1] Address to the Mathematical and Physical Section of the British Association, Brighton, 1872.

and the distance is afterwards measured as accurately as possible. Prof. Bond finds that the probable error of a similar measurement is 0″072 or ⅓ of the probable error of a similar measure made with a filer micrometer as estimated by Struve. Photographic pictures of the sun were for many years daily taken at Kew, and it was found that an extremely accurate measure of the sun's diameter could thus be made. If the lens of a common telescope were used to produce an image of the sun upon the sensitive plate the picture would be too small for accurate measurement. Hence a special instrument called a photoheliograph must be devised to give an enlarged picture upon the sensitive plate. Two perfectly distinct kinds of instruments are to be used for this purpose, the one English, the other American. Mr. Dallmeyer has, under the superintendence of Mr. De la Rue, constructed photoheliographs for the English and Russian expeditions. In these instruments the image of the sun produced in the focus of an ordinary telescope is enlarged by a special arrangement so as to give a picture of the sun about four inches in diameter. This instrument based upon the principle of the Kew photoheliograph, is very perfect in its results and convenient in actual practice. It is mounted equatorially so as to follow the motion of the sun. The sensitive plate, which is prepared in an adjoining room, can be readily inserted and exposed. The intensity of direct solar light is so great that special means are necessary to give a short enough exposure. Before a photograph is taken a sliding shutter in the interior of the instrument cuts off all light from the sensitive plate. This shutter is held in its place by a cotton thread. So soon as this thread is cut, a strong spring draws down the shutter, in which is a slit about $\frac{1}{40}$th of an inch wide. The time taken by this slit to pass over any part of the sun's image is the whole interval required for an exposure.

The other method of obtaining a large picture of the sun is by employing a lens of great focal length. This method was originally proposed by Mr. Rutherfurd, of New York, and will be employed by the Americans, and also by Lord Lindsay in his observations at the Mauritius. The focal length of the lens is forty feet. But a telescope of such dimensions could not be conveniently mounted in the ordinary way. To overcome this, a siderostat similar to the one originally constructed by M. Foucault for the Observatory of Paris is employed. This instrument consists of a plane mirror so mounted as to send the sun's rays always in the same horizontal direction. In the path of these rays, and close to the siderostat the lens is placed, and at a distance of forty feet an image of the sun about four inches in diameter is produced. At this place a window is arranged in a photographer's hut, and by means of this arrangement the photographer need never leave his dark room. After preparing a plate he places it in position at the window; when exposure has been made he may remove the plate and develop it.

Considerable advantage is likely to accrue by the employment of dry plates, which all diminish the labour of the photographer. Researches upon this matter have been undertaken by Prof. Vogel, in

Holstein, Col. Smysloff, at Wilna, and by Capt. Abney, at Chatham. The employment of a dry process prevents all danger from the shrinking of the collodion-film. Herr Paschen[1] and Mr. De la Rue have made experiments upon this point. The latter gentleman finds that all shrinkages take place in the thickness of the film, so that the measurements would not be affected by it. But the more convenient dry-plate process is undoubtedly safer. Judging from the data furnished by Mr. De la Rue, this photographic method will give results of the utmost value.

II. *The Heliometric Method.*—The exact measurement of the distances of the edges of Venus from opposite edges of the sun would enable us easily to determine what is required, viz., the distance between the centres of the sun and planet at a given time. But the ordinary astronomical means are useless in measurements of this magnitude. To obviate this, a special instrument, called a Heliometer, will be employed by the Germans and Russians, and by Lord Lindsay. This instrument was originally used for measuring the diameter of the sun. The object-glass of a common telescope is divided so as to form two semicircles. A screw adjustment allows us to slip one-half of the lens past the other one along their line of junction; a fine scale measures this displacement. When the two halves of this object-glass are relatively displaced, two images of the sun are seen overlapping. The distance between the two images is proportional to the relative displacement of the two halves of the object-glass. This instrument has been brought to a

---

[1] *Astronomische Nachrichten*, 1872, lxxix. 101.

state of great perfection by Mr. Repshold, of Hamburg. It is a very troublesome instrument to manipulate, and the corrections due to the influence of temperature are extremely difficult to apply. Yet with great care there is little doubt that very accurate measurements can be made. The nature of the measurements required to obtain the distance between the centres of Venus and the sun will readily be understood. The method has been most ably discussed by Lord Lindsay and Mr. Gill in the Monthly Notices of the R. A. S., November 1872. At the same time it is difficult to conceive that this direct method will give results of equal value with the methods hereafter described. In fact, an opposition of Mars would be expected to give equally good results; for the distance of Mars from a fixed star can be more accurately observed with a micrometer than the distance between the centres of Venus and the sun; and a larger number of observations could be made.

III. *The Method of Duration.*—The third method of determining the least distance between the centres of the sun and Venus is less direct than either of the preceding methods; but it has stood the test of a previous trial, and we cannot say but that it will be more satisfactory than the other methods in the coming transit. The method of duration closely resembles the method originally proposed by Halley. The duration of the transit, as viewed from two distinct stations, is accurately determined. But the difference in this duration is affected by choosing stations upon a different system. Nevertheless this method is frequently called Halley's method. His

method consisted in choosing two stations, so that during the transit the one should be moving eastward and the other westward. It is further essential for success that Venus should pass nearly along a diameter of the sun. In the method employed last century, the two stations were chosen—the one far north, and the other far south. On referring to Fig. 11 it will be seen that in each case Venus appears to pass along a chord of the sun. But in the one case this chord is further from the sun's centre, and consequently shorter than the other. The duration of the transit, so far as this effect is concerned, is directly proportional to the length of the chord traced out by Venus. Thus from observation we obtain the lengths of these chords; and by geometry we can deduce the least distance between the centres of the sun and Venus at each of the two stations, and hence we can determine the sun's parallax. Fig. 12 illustrates this point very clearly. The duration is determined by two distinct observations made at each station, the internal contact at ingress and the internal contact at egress. The time of an internal contact is the time at which Venus appears to be just wholly within the sun's disc. These two times must be accurately determined; they will be separated by an interval of nearly four hours. Fig. 12 represents the illuminated hemispheres of the globe at the time of ingress and at the time of egress respectively in 1874. At either of these epochs the sun will be visible from every place marked on the corresponding map. The sun will be vertical at the place occupying the centre of the map; at all stations near the edges of the map the sun will at that time be near the horizon. The point from which the phenomenon will be first observed is there indicated, and likewise the point at which it is last seen. Straight lines are drawn across each map, and the hours marked upon them indicate the time at which the phenomenon will be seen.

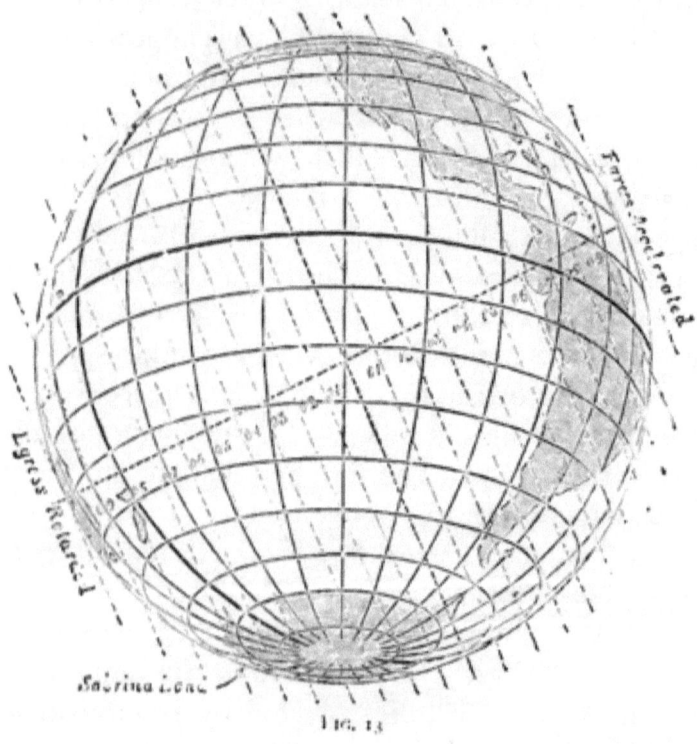

Figs. 13. 14. taken from a paper by the Astronomer Royal in the *Monthly Notices*, show the same facts for the transit of 1882.

Take now the case of two particular stations. At some point on the east coast of China the ingress is accelerated by 6 minutes, but at the same point the egress is retarded 7 minutes; consequently the duration of the transit is lengthened 13 minutes. Again, at Kerguelen's Island the ingress is retarded 10 minutes, while the egress is accelerated 5 minutes. Here then the duration of the transit is shortened 15 minutes. The difference in duration as observed

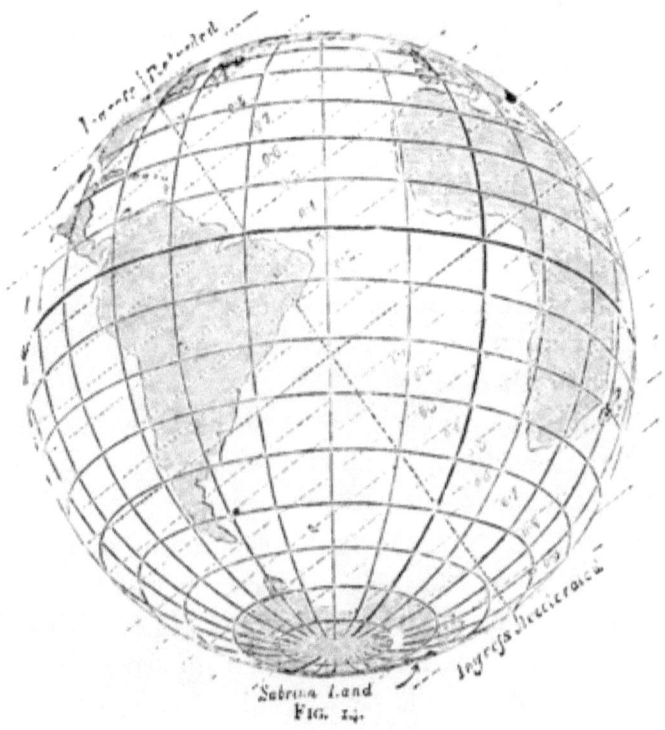

Fig. 14.

from these two stations will therefore be about 28 minutes. These maps have no pretension to great accuracy. They are calculated upon a certain assumption as to the value of the solar parallax which is probably not far from the truth.

In 1761 considerable preparations were made for

observing the transit of Venus in this manner. The English were represented by Messrs. Mason and Dixon at the Cape of Good Hope, and the French by the celebrated Pingré at the island of Rodriguez. A host of observers watched the phenomenon from northern regions. Unfortunately at scarcely a single station was the transit seen completely. Hence the method of durations was inapplicable, and another, originally proposed by De l'Isle,[1] came into use. This takes advantage of the fact that the ingress will take place later when seen from some parts of the earth than from other parts, as explained above; so with the egress of the planet from the sun's disc. Hence, if the absolute time of contact of Venus with the sun's edge at ingress or at egress be observed at two places suitably chosen, the difference in time will be a measure of Venus's parallax.

The method of De l'Isle will perhaps be better understood by looking upon the orbit of Venus as a vast protractor for measuring small angles. Venus moves, relatively to the earth, round the sun, that is through 360°, in 584 days. From this it follows that she passes over $1''\cdot5$ in one minute of time. Now conceive two straight lines to be drawn from the sun's edge, the one to the Sandwich Islands, where the ingress is most accelerated, and the other to Kerguelen's Island, where it is most retarded. Venus passes across these two lines like the radial arm of a protractor. The observed difference in the time of observing the phenomenon at these two stations will be about 21 minutes. Of this about 11 minutes is

[1] *L'istoire de l'Acad. des Sciences*, p 112.

due to the fact that the Sandwich Islands are north of Kerguelen's Island, as before explained; the remaining 10 minutes or so will be a measure of the angle between the two lines drawn from the sun's edge to the two stations. Since Venus passes over $1''\cdot5$ in 1 minute, 10 minutes gives us $15''$ for the effect of parallax looked at in this light.

It is a comparatively easy matter to set one's clock accurately to local time by astronomical observations. But it is a matter of considerable difficulty for an observer in Kerguelen's Island to set his clock accurately to the local time of the Sandwich Islands, or *vice versâ*. Consequently there will be some difficulty in determining the absolute difference of time of contact as observed at these two stations. The difficulty simply consists in determining the longitude accurately. This is a matter involving a long series of astronomical observations even now; still more so in 1761. Such observations were then wanting. Hence the application of this method was not successful, and results of that transit were unsatisfactory.

Not daunted by the comparative failure of that attempt, the astronomers of last century made vigorous efforts to make the transit of 1769 successful. The transit of 1761 was utilised in so far as it pointed out the difficulties in this kind of observation and gave them an approximate value of the sun's parallax to help them in choosing the most advantageous stations from which to observe the next transit.

Halley had no conception, when he proposed this kind of observation, of the difficulties attending it. The difficulty chiefly consists in determining accurately the exact instant when the contact seems to take place. The values which have been deduced from the observations of last century, and especially of the year 1761, have varied considerably according to the mode of reducing the observations. Thus in 1761, Lalande found, from the observations of Pingré, $9''\cdot 4$ for the solar parallax, while Maskelyne found from the work of Mason and Dixon $8''6$; Short[2] made it $8\cdot''65$; Wargentin, $8''\cdot 1$ to $8''\cdot 3$. Encke[3] showed that the differences were partly due to an error in the longitude of Rodriguez. This question will be capable of further discussion after this year, as Rodriguez is one of the stations chosen by the English from which to observe the coming transit.

Since the observers are likely to differ considerably in the manner in which they observe the contact, and since it is difficult for us to be sure that all observers have really actually noted the same phenomenon, photography is once more brought to our aid. Some time ago M. Janssen proposed a method for determining by the aid of photography the exact instant of contact. The value of his method was immediately recognised, and steps have been taken to utilise it. The method consists essentially in exposing different parts of a prepared photographic plate in succession to the sun's light, so as to photograph that portion of the sun's limb at which the planet is visible. By the aid of no very complicated mechanism a circular plate is so arranged that sixty different portions of its surface near the circumference are successively brought into

---

[1] *Phil. Trans.*, vol. lii. p. 647.   [2] *Ibid.* p. 648.
[3] *Zach. Corresp.*, ii. 1810, p. 367.

position, and exposed to the action of the sun's rays. The plate completes a revolution once in a minute, so that sixty photographs are taken at intervals of one second. A person who is observing with a telescope can easily give a signal to commence these photographic operations at the proper time. Thus one of the photographs will be sure to give us an indication of the time of true contact. Furthermore each one of the photographs taken at one station can be compared with a corresponding one taken at another station so as to give us a means of deducing the sun's parallax. The advantages of this method are enormous. The uncertainty which exists with respect to eye observations is in a great measure due to fluctuations arising from tremors in the instruments and variations in the density of the intervening air. In the photographic method, means have been taken to avoid these tremors as far as possible; and the instantaneous manner in which the photographs are taken will reduce these uncertainties to a minimum.

Various suggestions have been made as to the possibility of observing the exact time of the external contact by using a spectroscope in a beautiful manner originally devised by Mr. Lockyer and M. Janssen for observing the solar protuberances. Father Secchi has, in a very able memoir, pointed out a way by means of which this can be done; M. Zöllner has likewise pointed out the advantages of this method.

The observation of external contact is doubtless very useful as supplementary to the internal contact. The chief difficulty consists in the uncertainty of fixing the telescope in the proper position, so as to catch the exact point of the sun's limb. This difficulty would certainly be to a large extent obviated by the employment of the ingenious adjustable ring-slit devised by Lockyer and Seabroke. This device has, we believe, been already used with satisfactory results. It is much to be regretted that more observations to test its utility have not been made; as on this account it is not likely to be employed in the coming transit.

We have now completed the geometrical examination of the nature of the observations on the transit of Venus, by means of which the sun's parallax will be deduced. The complete examination of the question, including analytical methods, cannot be here dwelt upon. Anyone who is interested in this should consult the valuable work, "Les Passages de Vénus sur le Disque solaire," by M. Edmond du Bois, lately published, in which the theoretical part of the question is very fully investigated.

RECAPITULATION.—Before leaving the technical view of the matter it will be well to recapitulate what has hitherto been stated.

1. We know the *relative dimensions* of the solar system accurately; but we do not know the *scale*.

2. The determination of the distance of the earth from the sun or from any of the planets, at a fixed date, fixes the scale.

3. This may be determined (1) by the aid of a transit of Venus; (2) by an opposition of Mars; (3) by a knowledge of the velocity of light combined with observations of eclipses of Jupiter's satellites; (4) by

the velocity of light and the constant of aberration; (5) by the calculated effects of the sun's disturbance upon the lunar motions.

4. A transit of Venus may be utilised :—

    (*a*) By the determination of times of contact at different stations, combined with a knowledge of the longitudes of these stations.

    (*b*) By determining the least distance between the centres of the sun and Venus during the transit, observed from different stations.

5. This last determination may be made by any of these methods :—

    (1) The Photographic Method.
    (2) The Heliometric Method.
    (3) The Method of Durations.

CHAPTER IV.

It has already been pointed out how unsatisfactory in some respects were the results of the observations made in 1761. Those of the year 1769 were more successful, but the discrepancies of different observers still threw a doubt on the result. After Encke had discussed with all possible care the observations made upon these two occasions,[1] doubts were still raised as to the correctness of the value thus found for the solar parallax. The reasons of these doubts were manifold. In the first place, in order to get any value whatever of the solar parallax, Encke had been forced to assume that enormous errors had been committed by some of the observers; and again, all the other methods of which we have spoken were found to give a tolerably accordant value of the solar parallax, but values that differed considerably from Encke's determination.

It was with no small satisfaction then, that astronomers learnt that M. Powalky in 1864 had deduced a sensibly greater value for the solar parallax, by using more accurate values for the longitudes of the places of observation.

[1] *Berlin Abhandlungen,* 1835, pp. 295–310.

But Mr. E. J. Stone, now her Majesty's astronomer at the Cape of Good Hope, has lately re-discussed these observations.[1] He finds that, when the remarks of the observers are rightly interpreted, all the observations agree without any extravagant errors of observations; and moreover, the value of the solar parallax thus deduced agrees with the values found by other means. Mr. Stone deserves the thanks of the scientific world for having convinced them that this method, which at one time was falling into disrepute, may really be rendered very trustworthy.

The result of Encke's determination was that the mean distance of the sun from the earth is about 95 millions of miles. It now appears that the true distance is somewhere about $91\frac{1}{2}$ millions of miles. The annexed table gives the values of the sun's parallax and distance as determined by different methods.

Method.	Parallax.	Dist. of sun in miles.	Computer.
Transit of Venus[2]	8."91	91,580,000	Stone
Opposition of Mars	8."943	91,240,000	Stone
Lunar Theory[4]	8."010	91,520,000	Hansen
Lunar Theory[5]	8."850	92,200,000	Stone
Planetary Theory[6]	8."859	92,110,000	Leverrier
Jupiter's Satellites and velocity of light[7]	8."86	92,100,000	Foucault
Constant of Aberration and velocity of light[8]	8."86	92,100,000	Cornu

The uncertainty of observation which Mr. Stone aimed at clearing away is one of a very curious optical

---

[1] *Monthly Notices of the R. A. S.*, xxviii. p. 155.   [2] *Ibid.* xxvii. 255.
[3] *Ibid.* xxiii. 183.   [4] *Ibid.* xxiv. 8.
[5] *Ibid.* xxvii. 271.   [6] *Comptes Rendus*, July 22, 1872.
[7] *Ibid.* 1862, 1 502.   [8] *Ibid.* 1873, p. 341.

character. It is found that Venus at the time when she has almost completely entered within the sun's disc does not retain her round aspect, but becomes pear-shaped, or at least connected with the sun's limb by a "black drop" or "ligament." This ligament sometimes appears simply as a fine black thread connecting the planet with the limb of the sun. One observer in 1769 saw a number of black cones shooting out to the sun's edge in a fluctuating manner.

Many of these phenomena were doubtless due to bad definition of the telescope employed, or to the instability of its mounting. But the existence of a "black drop" even under the most favourable circumstances cannot be doubted; it was well observed in the case of a transit of Mercury that occurred in 1868.[1] If the planet be entering upon the solar disc, the first phase occurs when the edges of the sun and planet *seem* to be in contact. The second phase occurs at the instant when the "black drop" breaks off and a flood of light sweeps in between the planet and the sun. This occurs very suddenly, and has been supposed to indicate the true time of actual contact.

By referring to the *Philosophical Transactions* of 1769-70, a large number of descriptions of the phenomenon may be read. Some of the appearances are shown in Fig. 15, they are copied from the originals by Bevis, Hirst, Bayley, and Mayer, respectively—Prof. Grant states that the last one bears a resemblance to the appearance of Mercury as seen during its transit in 1868 from the Glasgow Observatory, the sun being near the horizon.

[1] *Monthly Notices*, xxix. p. 17, &c.

In the case of that transit of Mercury, studied by six experienced observers at Greenwich Observatory, two curious facts appear. Firstly, the times of contact as determined by different observers vary to the extent of 13½ seconds. And secondly, the shape of the planet varied considerably with different observers.

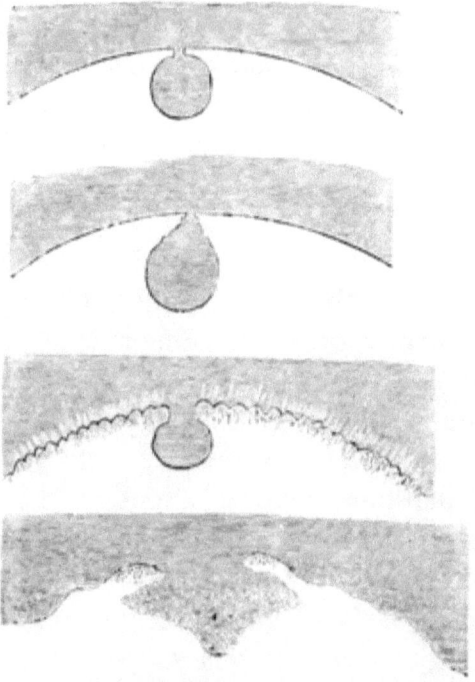

Fig. 15.—The "black drop," as observed in 1769.

Mr. Stone having noticed a confusion in the language of the astronomers of the last century as to which of the two phases was observed, carefully re-studied their words; and by supposing the two phases to be separated by a constant interval of time, he utilised both kinds of observation. This constant interval of time was deduced from all the observations, and found to be about 17 seconds. In this manner he arrived at the more accurate value of the sun's parallax.

It has been asserted that astronomers claim undue credit for the accuracy of their measurements, since Encke made an error of three or four millions of miles in the calculation of the sun's distance. This is not so. A chemist may be able to weigh many substances with an error of $\frac{1}{100}$ per cent. or less; but if the substance to be weighed be only $\frac{1}{100}$ of a milligramme, he might have a larger percentage error. When we consider how extremely small an angle the solar parallax is, it is astonishing to find so great a concordance between the results of different methods.

As to the cause of the phenomenon of the "black drop," Lalande ascribed it to irradiation. Irradiation is that curious phenomenon in virtue of which a star, or any bright object, appears larger than it really is. If a thin platinum wire be intensely heated by the passage of an electric current, it seems, to a person distant about fifty feet, to be as thick as a pencil. In this way the sun's diameter seems to be increased. The sun's light also encroaches upon the disc of the planet and makes it seem to be smaller than it really is. But when Venus and the sun have their edges almost in contact, as shown by the dotted line in Fig. 16, then there is no light at that point which can encroach; hence we see at this point the "black drop" to which allusion has been made.

Father Hell, one of the observers in 1769, ascribed the phenomenon of the "black drop" to the sensible size which an illuminated surface must have before it can be visible. There is probably some truth in each of these suppositions.

As to the cause of irradiation, it is difficult to speak with certainty. It is probably due in part to the telescope and in part to the eye. Great confusion has been introduced by persons neglecting to separate two perfectly distinct phenomena. True irradiation

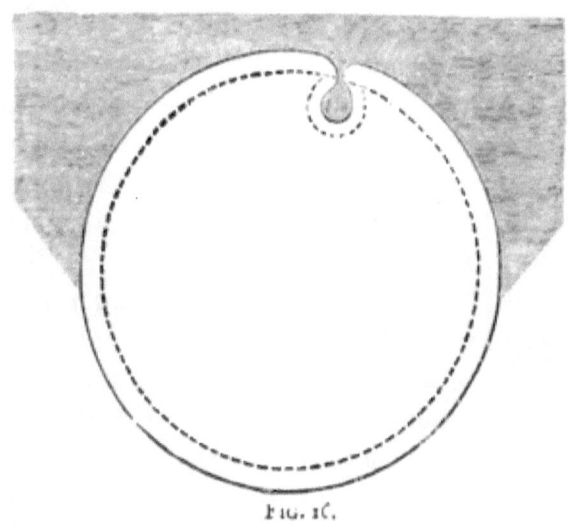

Fig. 16.

is only observed with a powerful light. With less illumination similar results may be seen, but they are of a different nature, and are produced between the formation of an image on the retina and its reception by the brain. In accordance with the customary nomenclature, this error of vision may be called the *mental aberration* of the eye. It is a perfectly definite phenomenon capable of accurate investigation, and M. Plateau has made measurements of the mental aberration of his own and his friends' eyes.[1] True

[1] Nouv. Mém. de l'Acad. Royale de Bruxelles, t. xi. p. 1, &c.

irradiation may be caused either wholly or in part by the spherical aberration or the chromatic aberration of the eye, or by diffraction, or by a spreading of the excitement of the nerves of the retina, which gives rise to the sensation of vision over a sensible space. In a telescope it is probably chiefly due to diffraction.

The success or failure of all observations of contact in the coming transit will to a great extent depend upon our knowledge of the nature of this appearance. For this reason numerous experiments have been made with the object of gaining information upon the question. The Russians, Germans, Americans, and English have all mounted artificial transits of Venus for the practice of observers. The arrangement adopted by the Astronomer-Royal consists essentially of a metal disc with two arcs of circles drawn upon it to represent the sun's edge with the metal between them cut away. Behind these there passes a glass plate with a circle of metal to represent Venus let into it flush with its surface. The glass plate is moved by clock-work so that the different phenomena are observed in succession exactly as they will be seen in the true transit. As the artificial planet passes in succession the two arcs representing the sun's edge, the phenomena of ingress and egress are successively observed. Before contact takes place, the sun has two cusps at the point of contact where Venus is touching the edge of the sun. The distance between the points of these cusps rapidly diminishes, the space between them being intensely black. They suddenly meet. But between the planet and the sun's edge a light shade is still seen which lasts several seconds before the planet appears completely detached. If instead of watching the meeting of the cusps, the part between them be studied, a sudden diminution of intensity of the blackness is seen about a second before the meeting of the cusps. The diminution of brightness is very sudden, and this is the phenomenon to be chiefly attended to in the actual observation. It occurs almost exactly at the moment of true contact, though the "black drop" does not disappear until some seconds later. It is of the utmost importance that the nature of these different phenomena should be carefully studied by all the observers. And at the present time experiments are being made with a view of determining the personal equation of each of the observers on the British expeditions.

But the actual observation will be rendered more difficult for various reasons. Firstly, the enormous extent of atmosphere which the rays of light must penetrate before reaching the telescope will destroy the definition to a large extent. Secondly, the existence of an atmosphere around the planet Venus may materially affect the nature of the phenomenon.

In any case there is little doubt that as many of the observers as possible of all countries should describe, as accurately as can be done, the exact appearances which are noticed at successive stages of the ingress and egress respectively. Comparisons being also made between different observers and between different telescopes, it will be possible to reduce the observation of any phase which may chance to be caught in the actual observation to the true time of contact. From observations with the Model Transit of Venus made at Greenwich, the following facts appear:—

1. It requires considerable experience for an observer to appreciate all the definite changes of appearance which occur.

2. When two observers describe a particular phase which they see, and determine to observe this phase together, the times recorded by each are generally accordant within a fraction of a second.

3. The successive phases of an ingress or egress appear to follow each other sometimes rapidly, at other times gradually; so that in some cases all the phenomena are observed within three seconds, on other occasions the same series of phases is completed in ten seconds.

4. The time at which any particular phase is observed varies very slightly with the aperture of the telescope. When a telescope of good definition is employed, the time of any phase at ingress is earlier than with an instrument of less perfect definition.

In the case of the observations of last century, it is easy to see how observers quite unprepared by previous observations as to the nature of the appearances they were about to witness were sometimes inconsistent with each other. In fact, without preliminary practice, and with bad definition, observers might vary even with a Model Transit of Venus by as much as 15 seconds. But, knowing what they are to observe, they would differ under no circumstances by more than about 2 seconds. Hence it is probable that in the actual transit, if the definition be good, the observation *may* be accurate to within one second; but if the circumstances be not very favourable, they may differ to an extent of fully three seconds, even after considerable practice with the model. These estimates serve to give us some idea of the accuracy with which we may hope to have the observations made; and it is probable, from the care which has been taken to multiply the number of observers at each station, that each pair of observations of contact will give us a determination of the parallax of the sun true to about $\frac{1}{3}$ per cent.

In the observations of contact, however, a great deal depends upon the experience of the observer; and it is fortunate that the idea originally thrown out by M. Janssen, and the mechanical execution of which has since been so ably carried out, will indelibly record the progress of the phenomenon and serve as a check to the observers.

By the aid of this method photographs of particular sun-spots have already been taken with great success at intervals of one second during one minute of time. Each of these sixty photographs is perfect in itself, and would admit of very perfect measurements. Hence there is every reason to believe that in this manner an independent and very valuable observation of the true time of contact will be made at each station where a photo-heliograph is situated.

The observations by means of photography during the progress of the transit have few difficulties to contend with. Their value will be largely increased by the fact that the actual measurements will be made afterwards when the observer cannot be carried away by the excitement of the moment. But even in this class of observation there are difficulties which must be carefully considered. It is found that if a sensitised plate be over-exposed, the image of the sun is considerably enlarged. This is due to *photographic irradiation*. It appears from experiments by Lord Lindsay and Mr. A. C. Ranyard to be mainly caused by the reflection of light from the back of the glass plate.[1] It can be almost entirely avoided by wetting the back of the plate, and placing black paper against it. There will still be probably a slight enlargement of the sun's diameter. This will not affect the relative positions of the centres of the sun and Venus; but it will render it extremely difficult to determine the unit of measurement.

There are two ways of applying the photographic method. The first is the same as the heliometric method. For this purpose it is necessary to have one station in the north and another in the south. By the other method we do not determine the distance between the sun and planet together with the exact time, but the actual position of the planet at each observation. In other words, we determine the distance of Venus's centre from the sun's centre, and also the angular distance measured from the north point of the sun. To do this we must have in the focus of the photo-heliograph a fine thread to indicate the direction of the meridian in the photograph; or in the American method we must have a thread suspended vertically which shall indicate the vertical direction in the solar photograph. The arrangements of the American method, as set up by Lord Lindsay at Dun Echt, are

[1] *Monthly Notices of the R.A.S.*, 1872, p. 513.

FIG. 17.—Lord Lindsay's Photographic arrangements as set up at Dun Echt.

shown in Fig. 17. The siderostat, lens, and hut, are all shown in position.

The value of the different methods has been well discussed by De la Rue,[1] Tennant,[2] and Proctor.[3] The method which takes into account the *actual* position of the planet on the sun is the more accurate, but it requires that the fiducial lines, or lines of reference, shall be exactly represented in the photographs. Mr. De la Rue says that this can be done to within one minute of space.

Besides photographic irradiation, however, there is a very important difficulty which enters into both the photographic and heliometric methods. This is due to the refraction of our atmosphere. Everyone knows the distorted forms which the sun assumes at the time of sunset. In our own climate these appearances are seldom seen on account of clouds and the haziness of the atmosphere. But even from a high mountain, or from any position which allows the form of the sun to be accurately seen up to the time of sunset, its shape may be noticed to be either square, elliptical, or pear-shaped, according to the circumstances of the atmosphere. Now at the most favourable points of observation the sun will be comparatively near to the horizon. Consequently its form will vary with the temperature of the air and with atmospheric disturbances. With our feeble knowledge of the laws of refraction it will be a matter of some difficulty to determine with accuracy the distance at different times between the centres of the sun and Venus.

---

[1] *Monthly Notices of the R. A. S.*, xxix. pp. 48 and 282.
[2] *Ibid.* 280.   [3] *ibid.* xxx. 62.

The same remarks apply to the heliometric method. But with stations chosen where the sun is not too low, we may expect accurate results. The value of a heliometer over other instruments designed for measuring small angles consists in this, that by it we can measure angles as large as the sun's diameter. It is expected by observers with this method that an observation will be made each time with an accuracy comparable with that of an observation of the time of contact. In this case the heliometric method will give valuable results. For the same reasons observations made by means of a double-image micrometer of the distance between the limbs of the sun and Venus near the time of contact will be as accurate as an observation of the contact itself.

The last difficulty which we shall mention in connection with this kind of observation is due to atmospheric conditions as affecting the apparent time of contact. With regard to the British expedition, great care has been taken to choose stations where the weather can be depended upon. But in cases where the method of duration is applied, the observations will be useless if there be not a very clear atmosphere both at ingress and at egress. De l'Isle's method, on the other hand, requires a perfect observation only at the time of one of these phases. Hence the nations which have adopted this method are less likely to be disappointed than others.

CHAPTER V.

It is probable that the observations of contact will be very materially supported by additional observations made with the double-image micrometer. This instrument was devised many years ago by Sir George Airy.[1] It is the most convenient eye-piece micrometer which can be used for measuring the distance between a pair of stars, or, as in the present case, between the limbs of the sun and Venus. The peculiarity of Airy's double-image micrometer consists in this, that one of the lenses forming an erecting eye-piece is divided in two, like the object-glass of a heliometer. The one half can be slid past the other, and the amount of displacement accurately measured by a divided circle on the screw which gives this motion. When the halves of this lens are relatively displaced, two images of the object are seen, as in the heliometer. If the distance between a pair of stars be the subject of measurement, the line of separation of the half-lenses is made to coincide with the line joining the two stars. The screw is

[1] Greenwich Observations, 1840.

now turned in one direction, until the image of one star given by one half of the lens coincides with the image of the other star given by the other half of the lens. The amount of displacement is then read off. The halves of the lens are again brought to coincidence. The screw is now turned in the opposite direction, and a similar observation made. Knowing the value of the divisions on the divided circle, these two observations give us a means not only of determining the distance between the two stars, but also of fixing accurately the reading of the instrument when the half-lenses are in coincidence.

It is easy to see that after the internal contact at ingress, and before the internal contact at egress, measurements may thus be made of the distance of Venus from the sun's limb, from which the true time of contact may be deduced, just as in the Janssen photographic method.

But, besides, this double-image micrometer gives a means of estimating the true time of contact in a manner which may possibly be one of very great accuracy indeed. Consider the case of ingress two minutes before the time of true contact. From this time up to the actual contact the distance between the cusps, where the limbs of Venus and the sun meet, will diminish with very great rapidity. By turning the micrometer so that the line of junction of the half-lenses is in a line with the points of these two cusps, the distance between them may be very accurately measured. The observation may be repeated a number of times. The great rapidity with which these cusps approach, with a very slight motion of the planet, makes it probable that each of these observations will give the means of determining very closely the true time of contact.

There are great difficulties connected with observations of the sun at such low altitudes as are required for the application of De l'Isle's and other methods. These will materially affect the definition of the cusps, and it is not certain that the micrometer method will give results so valuable as might have been anticipated.

But even in the eye-observation of contact the low altitude of the sun will be a serious drawback. This difficulty has been fully recognized by the Astronomer-Royal, and, with the assistance of Mr. Simms, he has devised an ingenious eye-piece, which is likely largely to reduce the inconvenience.[1] The chief difficulty is, that at such low altitudes not only are the rays of light enormously refracted by the earth's atmosphere, but the colours are actually dispersed, as with a prism. Hence the definition cannot be perfect. The principle of the new eye-piece consists in employing a lens next the eye, larger than is required for the pencil of rays falling on it, so that different parts of it can be used for different altitudes of the star. The surface of this lens next to the eye is plane ; and the lens can be moved, by means of a screw and slight spring, in a socket which is a portion of a sphere the same radius as the lens. By turning the screw, various inclinations can be given to the plane surface next the eye. But the curvature of the other surface remains the same, though a different portion of it is used.

[1] *Monthly Notices of the R.A.S.*, vol. xxx. p. 58.

The practical result, then, of such an inclination of the lens in its socket is simply the introduction of a prism whose angle can be so varied as to correct totally the atmospheric dispersion.

But in the case of photography the low altitude of the sun introduces a much more serious difficulty. The light has in this case to pass through a great length of the earth's atmosphere, in its lowest and densest regions. Much of the light is absorbed by the atmosphere, as is shown by the fact that the rising or setting sun may be gazed at with impunity. But further, it appears that of all the colours composing the sun's light, those which affect most powerfully a photographic plate are the most greedily absorbed. Hence it has been found at St. Petersburg that at mid-winter, when the altitude of the sun is about 6° or 7°, a photographic plate must be exposed to the sun 360 times as long as at the equinoxes. This is a difficulty which cannot be surmounted except by exposing the plate a longer time than is desirable.

It has been already stated that considerable discrepancies in determining the times of contact might arise from observers noting different phenomena. The employment of the Model Transit of Venus insures concordance among the observers of each nation; but all European observers will be much indebted to M. Struve, who has actually compared his own observations with those of the Russian, German, English, and French observers, so that comparisons will be possible between the results obtained by these different nations.

Everything being now prepared for observing as successfully as possible the actual phenomenon of contact, it remains to describe the means by which the time can be determined accurately. All clocks and watches are set and regulated by observations of the stars, or by comparison with other clocks so regulated. An astronomical clock counts the hour up to 24h. The clock is set to 0h. at the instant when a certain point in the heavens passes the meridian. If then we have a means of determining the time when this happens, we can set our clock accurately to local time. But a star does not pass the meridian of Greenwich at the same time as it passes the meridian of a place having any other longitude. By the aid of a transit instrument the local time can be determined; but to determine actual Greenwich time at another place we must, as before stated, know accurately the longitude of that station. *These two things, the Greenwich time and the longitude, are so connected, that if we know the one, the other can be immediately deduced from the local time by simple addition or subtraction.*

The longitude may be determined in a variety of different ways. If the two places whose difference of longitude is to be determined be not very distant, a simple method may be employed. A rocket is sent up from some point between the two stations. An observer at each station notes the local time at which the rocket is seen to burst. The difference between these times give the difference of longitude. A flash from a lamp, or reflected sunlight, may be similarly employed.

The Greenwich time (and consequently the longitude) can also be found by transporting chronometers from one station where it is known to another where it is not known. First-rate chronometers must be used, and a large number to check one another's errors. The main error of a chronometer is due to the influence of temperature on the momentum of the balance wheel and the strength of its spring. The Russians have of late years introduced with great success a method of secondary correction for this error. Along with the compensated chronometer at least one is sent without any compensation. The difference between this chronometer and others is a measure of the sum total of the temperatures to which they have been exposed; and by the aid of a table carefully drawn up from a number of observations, the amount of secondary correction necessary can be fairly estimated. It is said that the employment of this device is of the very greatest service. Ten well-tried chronometers, accompanied by a single uncompensated one, if carried between stations ten days apart (*e.g.* St. Petersburg and Cazan), will, in one journey, give the longitude of an intermediate station (such as Moscow) correctly within $\frac{1}{16}$ of a second of time. By the aid of this contrivance chronometers may be employed, even for very long journeys, to determine the longitude. This method is quite new, and has not been tested by any nation except the Russians. The results obtained by them are, however, perfectly satisfactory. Theoretically the idea is almost perfect; the outstanding temperature error being the main fault of chronometers, and the employment of an additional chronometer uncompensated giving us a means of determining the amount of this error, the time deduced by this means ought

F

to give very satisfactory results. There is but one objection to the method, which is only a partial one. After a series of alternately very hot days and very cold nights, the difference between the compensated and uncompensated chronometers might be the same as after the same period, with a tolerably uniform temperature; but the correction necessary in these two cases might be very different indeed. It is easy, however, to keep chronometers at a temperature which does not vary rapidly, and the experiments made by the Russians warrant us in saying that by the aid of this method longitudes may be determined, with very great accuracy indeed, in voyages of such length that the ordinary chronometric method would be unavailing, and that in every case where longitudes are required by the use of chronometers this method should be employed.

A third way of determining the absolute time is by the use of telegraphic signals. An operator at Greenwich may arrange to telegraph a signal to another at Alexandria at a certain definite time of day. If the transmission of the current from Greenwich to Alexandria were instantaneous, the person at Alexandria would at that instant receive the exact time. But a current through a submarine cable is retarded. Suppose it to be retarded two seconds; the time received at Alexandria will be *too late* by two seconds. If now an operator at Alexandria telegraphs to Greenwich he will despatch the signal two seconds *before* it reaches Greenwich. The longitudes determined by the two currents in opposite directions will therefore differ by four seconds. The mean of these values gives the true longitude, and half the difference between the two determinations is the time of transit of the currents. It is found, however, both from theory and experiment, that if there be a leak in the cable nearer to Greenwich than to Alexandria the current will pass more slowly in going to Alexandria than in the reverse direction; though this difference can never be very great.

Considerable differences have been found by the Americans to exist between comparative observations of longitude by the telegraphic method and by the lunar method, which will presently be described. The Americans rushed to the conclusion that the error existed in the lunar method. This is not necessarily so. The American system of telegraphing over long distances consists in using a *relay*. A relay is an arrangement to overcome the difficulty of sending a current through a long line. It is placed at an intermediate station. It consists essentially of an electro-magnet which attracts a piece of iron when a current which has originally been sent through the primary station passes through its coils. This attraction of a piece of iron makes contact with a new electric circuit with a separate battery, and so the current is passed on to the final station, or to a second relay. The piece of iron must move through a sensible distance before the second circuit is completed. It has hitherto been supposed that the time lost in employing a number of relays could be eliminated by sending the current in alternate directions as above described. This is certainly not the case. The time elapsing before contact is made by a relay depends upon the strength of the current. The strength of the current depends upon the length of the wire through which it is passing, and also upon the strength of the battery. Consider now the case of a relay at the junction of a long and short wire. The current passing through the long wire is weaker than the other. Hence if the current first pass through the short wire, the loss of time introduced by the relay is less than when the current is first sent through the long wire. For this reason the time taken by the current to pass in one direction is less than in the other direction. It appears then that the employment of a number of relays is injurious in longitude determinations, and if extraordinary precautions be not taken the resulting longitude will be erroneous. The same takes place with a submarine cable, with a leak near one end of it.

It must be noticed that in all the methods here described for determining the longitude, the local time must be accurately known. This is done by aid of a transit instrument as before described. One of the transit instruments of the British Expedition, in its wooden hut, is shown in Fig. 18.

Another class of methods for determining the longitude depends upon the motions of the moon. It has already been stated that what we want is to know at some instant the absolute Greenwich time. If then we could get something analogous to a huge clock in the heavens which an observer at any part of the world could see, we should be able to determine our longitude. The moon may be taken to represent the hand of such a clock, and the stars the hours and

FIG. 15.—The Transit-instrument of the British Expedition.

minutes. The moon is chosen in preference to the planets because she moves more rapidly among the stars. She moves around the earth, that is, through 360° in $27\frac{1}{2}$ days, or through 1° in two hours, or through one second of arc in two seconds of time. If then the tables in the *Nautical Almanac* predicting the place of the moon are absolutely correct, an observer, by watching the instant at which she seems to come to the position of any star, and knowing from the tables the Greenwich time at which she reaches that position, receives an intimation of the absolute time from this gigantic celestial clock. Or, if there be no star, it will suffice to observe the time when the moon reaches any definite position among the stars. As a matter of fact the tables of the moon are by no means perfect; but this difficulty is overcome by the regular series of observations of the moon's place made at Greenwich on every possible occasion. Thus while the tables are sufficiently accurate to give the navigator a fair knowledge of his longitude, an observer in any country can, when convenient, compare his observations with those made at Greenwich, and so determine the longitude with great accuracy.

It is a fact of interest in connection with the present subject, that the transits of Venus will aid materially in perfecting the Lunar Tables. The motions of the moon are rendered irregular by the disturbing attraction of the sun. But we cannot determine with great accuracy either the amount or the direction of the sun's attraction upon the moon until we know accurately the sun's distance. Hence if we wish to be able

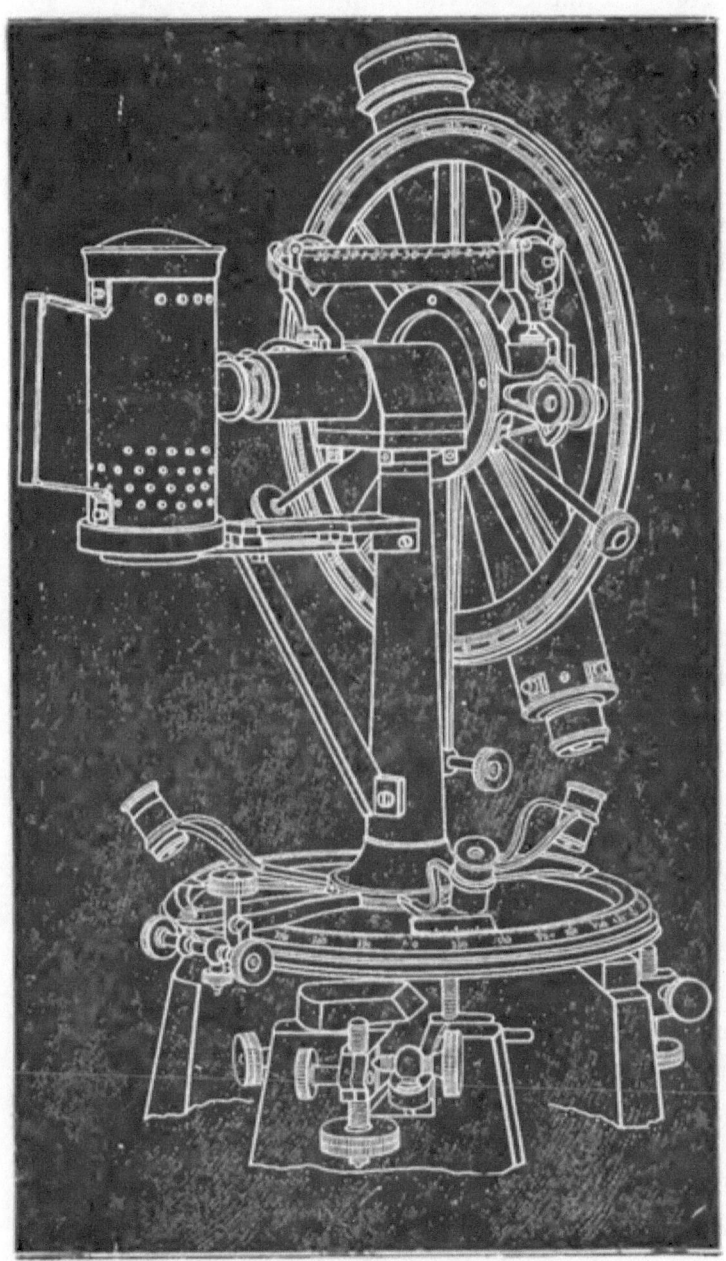

Fig. 19.—Portable Altazimuth Instrument.

to compute tables of the moon sufficiently correct for the exact determination of longitude, we must employ every means in our power to perfect our knowledge of the sun's distance.

Of the methods available for determining the moon's position, three will be employed in the coming transit. The first is by observing, with a powerful telescope, the exact time at which the moon extinguishes the light of a star in front of which it is passing. This is technically called an *occultation* of a star by the moon; and when the occultation is made by the non-illuminated portion of the moon the observation has great precision, and, the position of the star being known, is very valuable for determining longitude.

The second method is by observing, with the transit instrument, the exact time at which the moon passes the meridian, and by observing about the same time the transits of stars nearly in the same parallel whose positions are well known.

The third method is by employing an instrument called an altitude-and-azimuth instrument, or shortly, an altazimuth. One form of this instrument is shown in Fig. 19. It consists essentially of a telescope mounted upon two divided circles so arranged that the one shall give the altitude of an object towards which the telescope is pointing, while the other gives its azimuth or its angular distance from the meridian measured in a horizontal direction. An instrument of this class has long been employed at Greenwich with great success for determining the position of the moon when out of the meridian. It thus acts as a supplement to the transit-circle, of the utmost value in so cloudy a climate as our own. One disadvantage of this instrument is that the numerical reductions are extremely troublesome; but no trouble is too great in an observation of so much importance.

It is not absolutely necessary that both altitude and azimuth should be observed. In equatorial regions the motion of the moon is chiefly in altitude, while in places of high latitude in summer, when the moon is low, the motion is chiefly in azimuth. Hence among the English stations the vertical circles alone are provided for the stations within 30° of the equator, while at Kerguelen's Island and New Zealand the azimuth circles are accurately divided. All these instruments have been well tested, and are found to be remarkably perfect. Not only the altazimuths but also most of the other instruments to be employed by the British have been constructed by Troughton and Simms; they have all been well tried, and the results have been so satisfactory that these makers deserve great credit for the help they have thus given to the success of the expeditions.

In all observations of the moon for determining the longitude there are of course numerous corrections which must be applied. Among these none is more important than the correction for the parallax of the moon.

RECAPITULATION.—In the case of every nation depending upon De l'Isle's method, and in the case of every expedition when only one contact is observed, the longitude must be determined with very great accuracy. This can be done by any of the following methods :—

1. By rockets, or flashing signals.
2. By a trigonometrical survey.
3. By aid of chronometers, in which it would be unwise to neglect the method lately introduced of adding to the chronometers one which is uncompensated.
4. The telegraphic method, in which it is not desirable to use relays, since very long lines with a Thomson's reflecting galvanometer will give good results, while the employment of relays is objectionable.
5. By observations of the moon's position, which may be made by any of the three following methods :—
    (a) By occultations of the moon.
    (β) By transit observations of the moon and culminating stars.
    (γ) By aid of an altazimuth.

CHAPTER VI.

HAVING now discussed all the methods to be employed, and the chief difficulties to be encountered, it is time to examine what has actually been done. What method or methods ought to be chosen? What stations are most suitable, taking into account the chances of good or bad weather and good or bad anchorage? What preparations have been made by the various governments and by private individuals? And are the arrangements satisfactory?

As to the choice of method, the observation of contacts was the only kind originally contemplated. The employment of photography and heliometers is a comparatively new idea, and will be spoken of later. The observation of contacts is applicable to three methods, for each one of which different stations must be chosen; these are Halley's method, the method of durations, and De l'Isle's method. We will consider these in order.

1. Halley's method fails totally in the transit of 1874, but *may* perhaps be applied in 1882, though not under good conditions. On referring to Fig. 13 in

Chapter III., it will be noticed that Sabrina Land is a station where in 1882 the transit will commence just before sunset, and end just before sunrise. Hence during the transit this station and another located in America will be moving in opposite directions, thus fulfilling the conditions required by Halley in his communications to the Royal Society. By referring to Fig. 12 it will be seen that no such stations exist in 1874.

2. The method of durations may be successfully applied, so far as mere geometrical position is concerned, in either of the two transits. This method is really combined of two parts, and includes Halley's as a particular case. The lessening of the duration of the transit depends partly upon the diminished motion of one of the stations, or upon the fact that it moves in the opposite direction to the other; and partly on the fact that in one case the planet seems to trace a path on the sun further from his centre (and therefore shorter) than in the other. The difference in this last case is greatest when the path of Venus is far from the sun's centre. But in transits like the coming ones, where this is the case, the motion of Venus towards the sun's centre at the time of contact is very much slower than when she describes a large chord upon the sun. This has been well pointed out by Mr. Stone,[1] and from his paper we learn that the method of durations depending upon two such observations at each of the two stations will not be so satisfactory as we might otherwise have expected. But other very serious objections present themselves

[1] *Monthly Notices of the R.A.S.*, vol. xxix. p. 250.

to a method like this requiring four observations of contact, when we carefully consider the circumstances. In applying this method, one station must be chosen in high southern latitudes. Now diligent inquiries have been made upon this subject, and it appears very improbable that the weather at any suitable station will be such as to give much hope of observing both the ingress and egress in a satisfactory manner. Hence if we depended upon this method there would be a great probability of the expedition proving a failure. The method of De l'Isle requires the observation of only one contact at each of the two stations. For these reasons hardly any expedition will use this method except as secondary to De l'Isle's, the photographic, or the heliometric method.

3. De l'Isle's method. The accuracy with which this method can be applied depends upon the certainty of longitude operations. From what was said in the last chapter, it will be seen that this is no easy matter; but it is absolutely necessary that the longitude should be accurately found if this method is to be employed. Sir George Airy says that longitudes can be determined with an error of not more than one second by lunar observations; and observers will receive orders to remain at their stations until they have a sufficient number of observations to accomplish this. The lunar observations will be supported, where practicable, by telegraphic determinations of longitude, and also by the transport of chronometers. The Russians, whose stations lie mainly along the whole length of Siberia, will employ a telegraphic line over that region, with branch lines to the subsidiary stations. The

English will probably fix the longitude of Alexandria by submarine cable. They will employ chronometers to group together all neighbouring stations. The station at Rodriguez will be thus connected with Lord Lindsay's station at Mauritius, and with the Dutch station at Réunion. Lieut. Corbet, R.N., will connect by chronometers the various islands occupied by the Germans, Americans, and French in the neighbourhood of the two English stations on Kerguelen's Island. The three English stations on the Sandwich Islands will likewise be connected by chronometers; and it would be very desirable to connect these islands with San Francisco on the one hand, and Yokohama on the other. The longitudes of both these places will have been compared with Greenwich by telegraph. It would be a matter of the utmost interest to complete the chain round the world by the transport of chronometers across the Pacific. M. Struve says that with the aid of an uncompensated chronometer this might be done with great accuracy. The Germans have also made valuable suggestions for comparing the longitudes of the observing stations of all nations; and the French will also probably help in this matter. Thus it is likely that the longitudes of all the stations of different countries suitable for the application of De l'Isle's method will be very accurately known.

It will be noticed that the accuracy of De l'Isle's method depends upon two longitudes and two observations of contact; while that of durations depends upon four observations of contact. Neglecting all considerations of climate the two methods are, so far as the somewhat vague data at our command can tell us, very nearly equal. But the uncertain climate of southern seas renders the chance of many contact observations doubtful and throws the balance in favour of De l'Isle's method. Add to this that before long all the stations except the Kerguelen group will soon have their longitudes determined absolutely by telegraph, and recollecting that the coming observations are to serve astronomers until the next transit of Venus in 2004, by which time even the Kerguelen group may perhaps be chronometrically determined: recollecting all this, there is little doubt that astronomers have been wise in settling upon De l'Isle's method for the main observations of contacts.

It will be well, before going further, to mention the stations which have been chosen by different nations for the observation of the coming transit.

I. The British, having selected for the reasons above mentioned the method of De l'Isle, originally fixed upon the following stations :—

Alexandria, Sandwich Islands, Rodriguez, Kerguelen's Island, and New Zealand. No alteration has been made in the choice of these stations. Supplementary ones have, however, been added. Thus at Kerguelen's Island there will be two expeditions: one at Christmas Harbour in the north, and the other in the south of the island. In the Sandwich Islands there will be three stations: one at Honolulu, a second on the island of Hawaii, and a third on the island of Kauai, sometimes called by English writers Atooi. The station at Alexandria will be supplemented by a second one at Cairo, and a private one by Col. Campbell of Blythswood, under the Astronomer Royal's direction at Thebes. The New Zealand station will be placed at Christchurch. Since the idea of photography has been introduced, an additional station has been added by the Indian Government under the superintendence of Col. Tennant, R.E. This is very completely equipped, and will probably be situated near Roorkee.

Besides these the observatories at Madras, Cape of Good Hope, Melbourne, and Sydney will be utilised as far as possible. The New South Wales Government have voted 1,000*l.* for other observations in Australia. The English Government have voted 15,000*l.* for all the expeditions, but a much larger sum than this will be actually required. It will be understood that the principal method of observation is De l'Isle's, aided everywhere when possible by all the other methods except the heliometric.

From the account that has been given of the difficulty of determining the longitudes of the different stations it will be seen that no little power of organisation is required for the execution of the foregoing programme. All preparations must be made for the observation of the moon and moon culminators. Altazimuths must be made, and also actually invented for the express purpose. More than seventy chronometers must be provided, and negotiations must be completed with telegraph companies. The photographic operations have required the invention of a new photo-heliograph, and the Janssen method of a new application to it. The observations of contact have required the purchase of a large number of equatorials; for each station, besides having a 6-inch telescope, has also one or more smaller instruments. One of the larger ones, made by Simms, is shown in

FIG. 20.—6-Inch Equatorial of the British Expedition.

Fig. 20. The transit instruments have also been made expressly for this expedition. Besides this all the accessories of these instruments had to be provided. Huts for receiving them had to be made. Forms for entering and reducing the observations had to be prepared and printed. For some of the stations sleeping arrangements, cooking apparatus, washing utensils, and provisions had to be provided. Workmen, masons, and assistant photographers, besides twenty-two observers, had to be collected and trained to the work. When this is considered it will be seen that no ordinary man could fulfil all the duties. Fortunately we have in our Astronomer Royal a man who combines to an exceptional degree theoretical, mechanical, and organising powers; and we may safely say that the present expedition has been completed under a generalship quite unparalleled in the annals of Science. Sir George Airy has accomplished all that was required in a manner that has called forth the applause of those who have been connected with the preparations for this, perhaps the most important astronomical event of the century. We must congratulate ourselves upon the fact that he has been most liberally supported on all points by the British Admiralty. If we cannot enter into the same details with regard to other nations, it is only because we have not had the opportunity of learning all their actions. But we cannot conclude this account of the British Government expedition without alluding to the valuable services which have been rendered to it by Capt. G. L. Tupman, R.M.A., who has spent the last three years in training himself and nearly all the other observers in the use of the instruments, seeing the instructions of the Astronomer Royal carried out, ordering the stores, and in the most disinterested manner looking after the expedition; so that (as the Astronomer Royal has lately pointed out) if the observations be successful their success will in a great measure be due to his exertions.

II. Besides the expeditions under the direction of the British Government, another has been prepared which is perhaps the most completely equipped one which has ever been undertaken by a private individual in the interests of astronomy. Lord Lindsay has made preparations to take up his position at Mauritius, provided with means for utilising all the different modes of observation. He will combine his own results mainly with those of the Russians; and it is probable that no station could have been found more suitable for a single observer to occupy when so many different methods are employed. All the instruments are of the most perfect description and made by the best makers. The photographic method which he will employ has been already described. The siderostat has been made expressly for this purpose, and its surface has been tested and found to be truly plane. Lord Lindsay and his assistant, Mr. Gill, lay considerable stress on the employment of the heliometer, and have discussed its capabilities with great lucidity. They propose to make observations of the external contact by the aid of the spectroscopic method. The expedition will be provided with about 50 chronometers, including one uncompensated. These will be transmitted four times between Aden and Mauritius. It is probable that they will also connect the longitudes of the different stations on that group of islands by chronometers. The German expedition at Mauritius will probably be connected with Lord Lindsay's by a trigonometrical survey. Of these islands two can be connected by direct signals with a heliotrope reflecting the sun's light. From experiments made in Russia, it appears that a signal may thus be seen in a mountainous country with a clear atmosphere at a distance of 200 miles. There is little doubt then that the longitude of each station on this group of islands will be accurately known.

III. The Germans are sending out five or six expeditions. At Cheefoo the accelerated ingress and retarded egress will be observed; at Kerguelen Island the retarded ingress and the accelerated egress. The Auckland Islands will be favourable for accelerated egress; Mauritius for retarded ingress, and Ispahan for retarded egress.

They will probably employ all the four methods at most stations, viz. eye-observations of contact, heliometers, photo-heliographs for the distance of centres, and also for position-angles. There will be no photography at Mauritius. Here will be employed four heliometers by Fraunhofer, 3 in. aperture, $3\frac{1}{2}$ ft. focus; four equatorially-mounted telescopes by Fraunhofer, $4\frac{1}{2}$ in. aperture, 6 ft. focus; two photo-heliographs by Steinheil, $5\frac{1}{2}$ in. aperture, and two with quadruple object-glasses of 4 in. aperture. Besides these, instruments are required for determining the local time and the longitude; for the Germans lay great stress on De l'Isle's method. For this purpose transit instruments with diagonal telescopes on the Russian method of $2\frac{1}{2}$ in. aperture will be supplied, and altazimuths with divided circles 12 in. to 14 in. in diameter. The necessity of determining the longitudes accurately has led the German astronomers to consider carefully the best means by which this can be done. Dr. Auwers, to whom the direction of the arrangements has been intrusted, has discussed the matter in a very able manner. It appears from his inquiries that each group of stations will have their longitudes very accurately determined. Thus the stations in east Asia can be connected telegraphically. So also can those about Alexandria; also those about the Caspian Sea and New Zealand. The group of islands near Kerguelen's, the Sandwich Islands group, and the Mauritius group will be determined by chronometers. The only difficulty is to connect these different groups. Many of them will be compared with Greenwich indirectly by telegraph. It is probable that Honolulu will be compared by chronometers with San Francisco and Yokohama, thus completing, as already mentioned, the telegraph and chronometer connection round the world. In any case there is little doubt that before the transit of Venus in 2004 the longitude of Honolulu will be determined by telegraph. Since Lord Lindsay intends to compare the longitude of Mauritius with that of Aden by four chronometer expeditions, aided by an uncompensated chronometer, there is little doubt that the longitude of that group of islands will be accurately known. The group of islands about Kerguelen's will depend very much upon the British observations of the moon; but it will be well if chronometers can be employed to connect it with the Cape. The Germans rely very much upon the heliometric method. It will be a matter of great interest to learn how these observations agree with other methods as a guide to the arrangements for 1882. The expense of this expedition is about 130,000 thalers, besides the expenses connected with chronometric determinations.

The organisation of the German expedition has been entrusted almost wholly to Dr. Auwers, as secretary of the commission. His contributions to the subject are of great value, and the zeal with which he has superintended the expeditions, even in the minutest details, cannot be overvalued.

IV. The Russians are mainly employed in utilising the Siberian stations. The actual places which have been chosen from which to observe the transit are given in the following list, in order from east to west. The numeral 1 appended to a station means that there are good observers, practised with the model, good equatorials, and a heliometer or photo-heliograph. The numeral 2 signifies the same without heliometers or photo-heliographs. When the numeral 3 is appended, the observer has not practised with the model, and employs a small telescope. The stations are:

Yeddo 2	Blagowvschtchenska 2
Port St. Alga 3	Nertschinsk 1
Nakhodka 2	Xhita 1
Wladivostock 1	Kiachta 1
Port Possiet 1	Tomsk 3
Lake Hanka 1	Tachkent 1
Chabarovka 2	Port Peroffski 1
Peking 2	Fort Uralsk 1

Orenburg 3	Tiflis 3
Aschura-deh 1	Taganrok 3
Teheran 2	Kertch 2
Nachitzevan 2	Ialta 2
Erivan 1	Thebes 2

Besides these stations the following will be utilised, but the sun will be very low: Kazan, where the sun's altitude will be 8° or 10°; Nicolaif, where it will be 6°; and Charkof and Odessa 5°; at Moscow it will be exactly on the horizon.

As to instruments, the Russians are employing 6-inch and 4-inch equatorials. Their heliometers are larger than those of the Germans, having 4 in. apertures. Their photo-heliographs are constructed on the English model by Mr. Dallmeyer. The telegraphic connections between the stations have been already discussed. The expense incurred will be defrayed by the Government. Besides this, the State contributes 45,000 roubles. This will be spent mainly on the transport and maintenance of observers and instruments. The different observatories in Russia have shared the expense of providing the different instruments. The whole expedition has been conducted under the superintendence of M. Otto Struve. Some of the expeditions have already started provided with every means for resisting the cold of a Siberian winter. Great attention has been paid to the chances of good weather. The accelerated ingress and retarded egress will thus be admirably observed; and the comparison which M. Struve has made with observers of other countries in practising with the model will make it possible to reduce the results to the same standard. Moreover, many of the Russian stations are admirably situated for the employment of the method of durations; and if the two internal contacts be observed at any of the stations in the neighbourhood of Kerguelen's Island, excellent results may be obtained.

CHAPTER VII.

In our last chapter the preparations of Britain, Germany, and Russia were enumerated; those of the French, Americans, Dutch, and Italians must now be spoken of.

V. The French will occupy the following stations: —Yokohama, Peking, New Amsterdam or St. Paul's, and Campbell Island; all equipped as first-class stations, besides Tientsin, Sagou, Numea, and probably Nukahiva in the Marquesas, as secondary stations. Yokohama and St. Paul's will make an excellent combination for the method of durations; at Campbell Island also the durations will be considerably lessened. But the longitude of these places will be determined, so that if only one contact be observed, De l'Isle's method will be applied. MM. Wolf and André have made a series of experiments on the formation of the "black drop;" numerous trials have also been made with a view of employing the photographic method as successfully as possible, and it is possible that spectroscopic observations of external contact will be made. The preparations are by no means so far advanced as might have been wished. This is partly due to the disturbed state in which the country has been since the late war.

We are glad to be able to state that the French will employ the daguerreotype process of photography. This method has many advantages, and it is much to be regretted that no experiments have been made by other nations to test its applicability. Photographs taken by this process are well known to be much more delicate and give clearer details than any others, while photographic irradiation is reduced to a minimum. It is even possible to correct for curvature of field by employing prepared plates whose surfaces are portions of spheres, a thing which would be impossible by any other process. There can be no shrinking of the film. The only objection is, that we cannot print copies from the plates conveniently. But it is not likely that we should trust to measurements of a printed copy even from a glass negative. The French are relying mainly upon the photographic method, and have chosen their stations for determining thus directly the least distance between the centre of the sun and Venus. With the apparatus proposed by MM. Wolf and Martin, the size of the sun's image will be 60 millimetres; they hope to determine the instants of internal contacts with a probable error of one second of time. The commission into whose hands the business has been intrusted has drawn up a detailed report containing contributions not only from the astronomers of France, but also from the most celebrated physicists and experimentalists: 300,000 fr. has been voted for the enterprise. M. Tisserand of the Toulouse Observatory will aid in the actual observations; and M. Janssen will proceed to Yokohama.

M. Dumas takes the lead in the preparations. In a letter dated May 12, he says that the expeditions are on the point of starting, and that the Marquesas probably, and Numea certainly, will be occupied for De l'Isle's method.

VI. The Americans have a grant of 150,000 dols. They have paid great attention to the application of photography with the assistance of Mr. Rutherford, whose success in photographing the moon is so well known. They employ a lens of 40 ft. focus, as already described. They will measure both angles of position and distances from the centre, and the probable error of any measurement will be less than $\frac{1}{100}$ per cent. They have encountered some trouble in the manufacture of their siderostats. Besides photography eye-observations of contact will also be made. A very able report has been drawn up from the computations of Mr. Hill, who deserves great credit for the manner in which he has completed it. This report has reference to the choice of stations; and is accompanied by very valuable charts. Other reports have been made upon the application of photography.

The expeditions are to be composed of five persons each. The stations of observation and the heads of parties are as follows:—Wladivostock, Siberia,

Prof. A. Hall, U.S.N.; Nagasaki, Japan, Mr. G. Davidson, U S. Coast Survey; Peking, China, Prof. James C. Watson; Crozet's Island, South Indian Ocean, Capt. Raymond, U.S.A.; Kerguelen's Island, South Indian Ocean, Lieut.-Commander George P. Ryan, U.S.N.; Hobart Town, Tasmania, Prof. W. N. Harkness, U.S.N.; New Zealand, Prof. C. H. Peters; and Chatham Island, South Pacific, Mr. Edwin Smith, U.S. Coast Survey.

The whole organisation has been intrusted to a commission, the secretary of which is Prof. Newcomb, who has done so much valuable work for astronomy, and who has taken great pains to insure success for the expedition.

VII. The Italians have arranged to send out three expeditions furnished with spectroscopes for the observation of external contact. Little is known about these expeditions.

VIII. The Dutch are sending one expedition to the island of Bourbon or Réunion. It will be furnished with a photo-heliograph, which Dr. Kaiser will manipulate; Dr. Oudemans will also make observations with a heliometer.

Having now completed our description of the details, and having also given an account, so far as possible, of the preparations of the various nations for the observations, we shall cast a general view over the whole subject, and recapitulate some of the principal points.

The coming transit of Venus will be observed from about 75 stations, at many of which there will be a large number of instruments. The expense of the whole of the expeditions will amount to between 150,000*l.* and 200,000*l.* It may seem to some that the results to be arrived at are not worth so great an outlay, but the general voice of the non-scientific as well as of the scientific world has contradicted this. Wherever knowledge can be gained it is worth being gained ; and when individuals are unable to bear the cost, it is fitting that the expenses should be incurred by those governments that are really the gainers from many scientific researches for which the investigator himself frequently receives no reward. But apart from this, these expeditions will lead to most valuable results. The sun's distance being known, the Lunar Theory may be vastly improved, and it will be possible to determine longitudes with much greater accuracy than at present. Still more will the tables of Venus be capable of readjustment. Even now we can calculate her place with great accuracy, and this is fortunate, since it enables us to predict the exact time at which Venus will first come in contact with the sun, viz. 1874, Dec. 8d. 14h. 4m. The error to which this is liable, owing to the tables, is not likely to exceed five minutes. Mr. W. H. M. Christie, Chief Assistant of the Royal Observatory, has determined the probable error in the calculated time of contact arising from this cause.[1] He has employed observations of Venus taken at this node at the following dates:—1872, June 28 ; 1873, Jan. 18 ; 1873, Sept. 14 ; and 1874, April 25 ; he has thence deduced the error in the tabular position of Venus, and from this the error in the time of contact

[1] *Monthly Notices of the R. A. S.*, xxxiv. 300.

in the coming transit. It appears from each of these four comparisons that the tables of Venus give us the time of contact too early; according as we adopt the first, second, third, or fourth of the above observations, the error will be 7·4m., 5·3m., 4·2m., or 8·1m.

Besides the astronomical advantages to be gained from the coming transit, there are several collateral issues of no small importance. In the first place, the longitudes of a host of stations all over the globe will be accurately determined, and it is a remark by no means unworthy of notice that the simple observation of the local time of contact will give the inhabitants of east Africa and of all Asia an accurate means of determining their absolute longitudes. If, moreover, as has been proposed, San Francisco and Japan are to be compared directly as to longitude, the whole circuit of the globe will be completed by telegraphic and accurate chronometric determinations.

Again, with the host of vessels by which scientific men will proceed to their stations, meteorological, and sometimes even magnetical, instruments will be provided. These vessels will be traversing the different oceans of the globe about the same time, and thus the meteorology of the world will be much better understood. Many observers will be enabled to take note of interesting phenomena, such as hurricanes, volcanoes, and earthquakes. In addition, naturalists will be appointed to accompany some of the expeditions; birds and marine animals will be probably very generally collected; the Royal Society has given funds to aid in this matter. The Rev. A. E. Eaton, who has made valuable collections at Spitzbergen, will examine the marine life of Kerguelen's Island. Rodriguez is particularly interesting from a naturalist's point of view; it is one of the few islands in mid-ocean which have not been raised by volcanic agency. The remains of some extinct birds have been found there. The Royal Society has appointed a geologist, a botanist, and a naturalist to go to this island. There is little doubt that Science in general will gain greatly by these expeditions.

As to the main observation we can have no doubt, from the large number of expeditions, and from the multiplicity of methods to be employed, that we shall obtain excellent results, although the actual reduction of the observations will be exceedingly laborious. Each nation, while it generally adopts some special method for its choice of stations, will also utilise other methods. We have seen that the English, while they rely chiefly on De l'Isle's method, will employ all the others except the heliometric, while the Germans depend mainly upon the heliometric method. The French and Americans have chosen their stations with reference to photography. The Russians are to compare observations of all kinds with different nations. These countries have all co-operated in the most harmonious manner, partly by correspondence, and partly by the personal visits of astronomers to different nations.

Although the observations are to be made at the end of the present year, the actual reduction of the observations will take so long that we cannot hope for the complete and final results as to our distance from the sun before the year 1876. At each of the British stations the observers will remain at least three months to determine their longitudes.

Here we may leave the subject. The preparations are for the most part completed; many of the observers of different nations are on their way to their various posts. It says a great deal for the civilisation of the world that on December 8 of the present year those quarters of the globe will be thickly studded with emissaries from so many nations to observe an important astronomical phenomenon.

It will be well to conclude this account with a statement of the arrangements which have been made as to observers on the British expeditions. It is extracted from instructions published under authority:—

Appointments of Observers to the several Districts of Observation, and Subordination of Observers.

1. Capt. G. L. Tupman, R.M.A., is head of the entire enterprise, and is responsible through the Astronomer Royal to the Government for every part. Every observer is responsible to Capt. Tupman.

2. When the different expeditions are separated, the observers in each district of observation are responsible to the local chief of the district, and the chief to the Astronomer Royal. The districts of observation and the observers will be the following, the name first following that of the local chief being

Fig. 21.—Photo-heliograph of the British Expeditions.

that of the deputy, who will, if necessary, take his place :—

3. District A. Egypt : Chief, Capt. C. O. Browne, R.A., astronomer; Observers, Capt. W. de W. Abney, R.E., astronomer and photographer; S. Hunter, astronomer.

4. District B. Sandwich Islands : General Chief, Capt. G. L. Tupman, R.M.A.: Deputy, if necessary, Prof. G. Forbes.

Sub-divisions of the Sandwich Islands :—Honolulu: Chief, Capt. G. L. Tupman, astronomer ; Observers, J. W. Nichol, astronomer and photographer; Lieut. F. E. Ramsden, R.N., astronomer and photographer. Hawaii: Chief, Prof. G. Forbes, astronomer; Observer, H. G. Barnacle, astronomer. Kauai: Chief, R. Johnson, astronomer; Observer, Lieut. E. J. W. Noble, R.M.A., astronomer.

5. District C. Rodriguez : Chief, Lieut. C. B. Neate, R.N., astronomer; Observers, C. E. Burton, astronomer and photographer ; Lieut. R. Hoggan, R.N., astronomer and photographer.

6. District D. Christchurch (New Zealand) : Chief, Major H. Palmer, R.E.; Observers, Lieut. L. Darwin, R.E., astronomer and photographer ; Lieut. H. Crawford, R.N., astronomer.

7. District E. Kerguelen Island : General Chief, Rev. S. J. Perry ; Deputy, if necessary, Lieut. C. Corbet, R.N.

Sub-divisions of the Kerguelen Island :—Christmas Harbour : Chief, Rev. S. J. Perry, astronomer and photographer ; Observers, Rev. W. Sidgreaves, astronomer ; Lieut. S. Goodridge, R.N., astronomer ; J. B.

Smith, astronomer and photographer. Port Palliser: Chief, Lieut. C. Corbet, R.N.; Observer, Lieut. G. E. Coke, R.N.

8. In addition to these gentlemen, three non-commissioned officers or privates of the corps of Royal Engineers will be attached to each of the five districts, and will be under the direction of the chief of each district.

THE END.

SCIENCE PRIMERS,

UNDER THE JOINT EDITORSHIP OF

PROFESSORS HUXLEY, ROSCOE, AND BALFOUR STEWART.

"They are wonderfully clear and lucid in their instruction, simple in style, and admirable in plan." — *Educational Times.*

The following are now Ready: —

CHEMISTRY. By H. E. ROSCOE, F.R.S., Professor of Chemistry in Owens College, Manchester. Third Edition. 18mo. cloth.. Illustrated. 1s.

PHYSICS. By BALFOUR STEWART, F.R.S., Professor of Natural Philosophy in Owens College, Manchester. Second Edition. 18mo. cloth. Illustrated. 1s.

PHYSICAL GEOGRAPHY. By A. GEIKIE, F.R.S., Murchison Professor of Geology and Mineralogy at Edinburgh. Second Edition. 18mo. cloth. Illustrated. 1s.

GEOLOGY. By Professor GEIKIE. F.R.S. With numerous Illustrations. 18mo. cloth. 1s.

PHYSIOLOGY. By MICHAEL FOSTER, M.D., F.R.S. Illustrated. 18mo. cloth. 1s.

In Preparation:—

INTRODUCTORY. By Professor HUXLEY, F.R.S.

BOTANY. By J. D. HOOKER, C.B., F.R.S., President of the Royal Society.

ASTRONOMY. By J. NORMAN LOCKYER, F.R.S.

MACMILLAN AND CO., LONDON.

SCIENCE CLASS-BOOKS.

ANATOMY. — ELEMENTARY LESSONS IN ANATOMY. By St. George Mivart, F.R.S. With numerous Illustrations. 18mo. 6s. 6d.

ASTRONOMY.—POPULAR ASTRONOMY. With Illustrations. By Sir G. B. Airy, Astronomer-Royal. New Edition. 18mo. 4s. 6d.

ASTRONOMY.—ELEMENTARY LESSONS IN ASTRONOMY. With Illustrations. By J. Norman-Lockyer, F.R.S. With Coloured Diagram of the Spectra of the Sun, Stars, and Nebulæ. New Edition. 18mo. 5s. 6d.—Questions on the Same, 1s. 6d.

BOTANY. — LESSONS IN ELEMENTARY BOTANY. With Illustrations. By Professor Oliver, F.R.S., F.L.S. New Edition. 18mo. 4s. 6d.

CHEMISTRY.—LESSONS IN ELEMENTARY CHEMISTRY. By Professor Roscoe, F.R.S. With numerous Illustrations and Chromo-lithographs of the Solar Spectra. New Edition. 18mo. 4s. 6d.

CHEMISTRY.— OWENS COLLEGE JUNIOR COURSE OF PRACTICAL CHEMISTRY. By F. Jones. With Preface by Professor Roscoe. New Edition. 18mo. 2s. 6d.

LOGIC.—ELEMENTARY LESSONS IN LOGIC, Deductive and Inductive. By Professor Jevons, F.R.S. With Copious Questions and Examples, and a Vocabulary of Logical Terms. New Edition. 18mo. 3s. 6d.

PHYSIOLOGY.—LESSONS IN ELEMENTARY PHYSIOLOGY. With numerous Illustrations. By Professor Huxley, F.R.S. New Edition. 18mo. 4s. 6d.—Questions on the Same, 1s. 6d.

POLITICAL ECONOMY FOR BEGINNERS. By Millicent Garrett Fawcett. With Questions. New Edition. 18mo. 2s. 6d.

PHYSICS. — LESSONS IN ELEMENTARY PHYSICS. By Balfour Stewart, F.R.S., Professor of Natural Philosophy in Owens College, Manchester. With Coloured Diagram and numerous Illustrations. New Edition. 18mo. 4s. 6d.

STEAM.—AN ELEMENTARY TREATISE ON STEAM. By J. Perry, B.E., Whitworth Scholar, late Lecturer in Physics at Clifton College. With Illustrations, Numerical Examples, and Exercises. 18mo. 4s. 6d.

** Others to follow.

MACMILLAN AND CO., LONDON.

www.ingramcontent.com/pod-product-compliance
Lightning Source LLC
Chambersburg PA
CBHW022148160426
43197CB00009B/1474